READING
WALKER PERCY'S
NOVELS

READING WALKER PERCY'S NOVELS

Jessica Hooten Wilson

Louisiana State University Press
Baton Rouge

Published by Louisiana State University Press
Copyright © 2018 by Louisiana State University Press
All rights reserved
Manufactured in the United States of America

Designer: Laura Roubique Gleason
Typeface: Whitman
Printer and binder: LSI

Library of Congress Cataloging-in-Publication Data

Names: Wilson, Jessica Hooten author.
Title: Reading Walker Percy's novels / Jessica Hooten Wilson.
Description: Baton Rouge : Louisiana State University Press, 2018. | Includes bibliographical references and index.
Identifiers: LCCN 2017037458 | ISBN 978-0-8071-6877-6 (pbk. : alk. paper) | ISBN 978-0-8071-6878-3 (pdf) | ISBN 978-0-8071-6879-0 (epub)
Subjects: LCSH: Percy, Walker, 1916-1990—Criticism and interpretation.
Classification: LCC PS3566.E6912 Z974 2018 | DDC 813/.54—dc23
LC record available at https://lccn.loc.gov/2017037458

The paper in this book meets the guidelines for permanence and durability of the Committee on Production Guidelines for Book Longevity of the Council on Library Resources. ∞

To Brett Foster, who left behind
too many unfinished symphonies

CONTENTS

Acknowledgments	ix
Abbreviations for Works by Walker Percy	xi
Introduction: A Brief Biography	1
1. *The Moviegoer*	18
2. *The Last Gentleman*	36
3. *Love in the Ruins*	53
4. *Lancelot*	71
5. *The Second Coming*	88
6. *The Thanatos Syndrome*	107
Appendix: *Lost in the Cosmos*	123
Notes	135
Bibliography	145
Index	151

ACKNOWLEDGMENTS

In writing this guide to reading Walker Percy's novels I must be upfront in acknowledging all the many guides who helped bring this book to publication. First, my editor, Margaret Lovecraft, deserves the bulk of my gratitude, for the idea and invitation came from her. Second, thank you, Farrell O'Gorman, for being a secret admirer and passing my name on to her. I should thank all of the Dead Mules—Collin Messer, Douglas Mitchell, and Richard Russell—for allowing me to crash your various reunions at conferences across the country where I could overhear your insightful readings of Walker Percy and deliver them to readers in this guide.

Thank you, John Brown University, for granting me a Summer Scholars stipend in order to compose this manuscript. For all the readers who helped copyedit the original drafts, thank you: Ryan Madison, Becky Watts, Brad Gambill, Anna Nichols, and Ciera Nash. Also, I have not forgotten my 2014–15 Integrative Humanities students who walked through *Lost in the Cosmos* with me as I prepared the appendix of this book. Thank you to my university community for all the various ways you supported this project.

In addition to all these direct contributors, Rod Dreher and the group who puts on the Walker Percy Weekend in St. Francisville, Louisiana, ought to receive recognition, for it was this event that initially made me mindful of my audience and from whom I learned so much about reading Percy's novels.

Finally, my family must be thanked profusely for every book I write. They are the ones who miss me during the summer and who sacrifice the time on Saturdays and evenings for me to fulfill my vocation as a writer. Thank you to Jonathon, Evie, Zade, and Lucette for being such examples of generosity and selflessness to me. You guide me in the good life.

ABBREVIATIONS FOR WORKS BY WALKER PERCY

Correspondence   *Correspondence of Shelby Foote and Walker Percy.* Ed. Jay Tolson. W. W. Norton & Co., 1997.

L   *Lancelot.* New York: Farrar, Straus and Giroux, 1977.

LG   *The Last Gentleman.* New York: Farrar, Straus and Giroux, 1966.

LIC   *Lost in the Cosmos: The Last Self-Help Book.* New York: Picador, 2000.

LIR   *Love in the Ruins.* New York: Farrar, Straus and Giroux, 1971.

MG   *The Moviegoer.* New York: Random House, Inc., 1961.

MIB   *The Message in the Bottle.* New York: Farrar, Straus and Giroux, 2000.

SG   *The Second Coming.* New York: Picador, 1999.

Signposts   *Signposts in a Strange Land.* Ed. with an introduction by Patrick Samway. New York: Farrar, Straus and Giroux, 1991.

TS   *The Thanatos Syndrome.* New York: Picador, 1999.

READING
WALKER PERCY'S
NOVELS

INTRODUCTION
A Brief Biography

For the inaugural Walker Percy Festival in St. Francisville, Louisiana, on June 6–7, 2014, tickets sold out within weeks. A great many people who love Percy were attracted to the idea of driving hundreds of miles to eat crawfish and drink bourbon in his honor. Few of these were professors; they were from all walks of life: lawyers, bankers, clergymen, editors, honeymooners, homeschoolers, retirees, architects, artists, entrepreneurs, and homemakers, showing Percy's continuous appeal outside of universities. One of Percy's daughters, Mary Pratt Percy Lobdell, attended. She remarked, "This is so Daddy. He would have loved it. He would have been sitting there on the porch sipping his drink watching the rest of us sweat and laughing."[1] One could picture Percy enjoying the festivities, lounging in his button-up shirt, with his receding hairline and wide grin. What an author who fifty years after he published his first novel could still inspire flocks of people to congregate under the sparse shade of timeless oak trees in his ancestral Feliciana Parish and talk about returns, rotations, and the malaise, as though those ideas were commonplace. And, as much as Percy affected those around him while he lived, so the spirit of Percy embodied in his work continues to move strangers, as this gathering attested. So, who was Walker Percy, and why does his work continue to matter so much to so many? Let me offer a brief biography assembled primarily from the information in Jay Tolson's and Father Patrick Samway's extensive biographies, as well as Bertram Wyatt-Brown's *The House of Percy*.

Walker Percy comes from a long line of prominent Percys, possibly with origins as far back as the famous Percys of Northumberland, who graced the pages of Shakespeare's histories. For a twenty-first-century reader, trying to understand the influence of a traceable ancestry on a person seems as distant and foreign of an idea as the British monarchy.

It seems just as outdated of a notion and just as impotent. Nowadays, as another writer recently noted, the question, *where are you from?* is often too complicated to answer.² Rarely is someone "from" any one place any longer. Yet, Percy was not only *from* the South, and remained there most of his life, but so were his parents, grandparents, his grandparents' parents, and so on. Father Patrick Samway begins his biography of Percy with the aphorism that "anyone who grows up in the Mississippi delta knows the anecdotal history of 1200 people."³ Of that twelve hundred, at least a thousand appear connected to the Percy line. This great legacy could be a burden, a privilege, or a responsibility, but, for Percy, it was not merely a bit of genealogical trivia; it affected who he was and the stories that he told.⁴

From West Feliciana Parish across the Mississippi Delta to Birmingham, Alabama, the Percy family reigned for over two centuries, beginning with Charles Percy, who established a large indigo plantation near St. Francisville in 1785. In the front matter of *The Thanatos Syndrome*, his last novel, Percy created an imaginary Feliciana Parish that bears much resemblance to the West Feliciana Parish of his ancestors. A refuge for an assortment of malcontents, this Feliciana Parish is as "pleasant a place as its name implies." These pleasantries include LSU football, reruns of *M*A*S*H*, Dixie beer, and gumbo. Unfortunately, the modern world has taken its toll on the natural beauty that once characterized Feliciana—cutting down its pine forests, befouling its bayous, and making the Mississippi River into a veritable sewer. This pollution is only darkened by the increase in malls, chiropractic offices, and condominium complexes with French-sounding names. Yet, Percy, referring to Louisiana in general, insists, "I wouldn't live anywhere else."⁵ Shortly after his marriage, Percy settled down in Covington, Louisiana, where he lived until he died. His invented Feliciana Parish, however, shares much with the place where Percy's ancestors first established themselves; it became the backdrop for many of his stories.

The eighteenth-century Louisiana that Percy describes in the opening of *The Thanatos Syndrome* would have been what greeted the avantgarde "Don Carlos" Percy in America, so titled for his brief stint as a magistrate to the recently disposed Spanish. Little is known about this founding Percy, this wayfarer from the Old World. Although he claimed to be from the famous Percys of Northumberland, he could as easily have been a pirate, a convict, or a stowaway.[6] One of his famous descendants, the twentieth-century poet William Alexander Percy (also Walker Percy's adopted father), depicts him issuing out of the sea "like the Flying Dutchman or Aphrodite."[7] There are no records of his existence prior to coming ashore on the coast of Florida in 1775.[8] With a bold tale of how he lost all of his prior belongings, he received a land grant of nearly one thousand acres in Louisiana and began accumulating more. Like other southern families of the time who wanted to glory in their European aristocratic roots, Percy named his plantation "Northumberland House."

Such claims of previous high class were usually false in the South, as W. J. Cash reveals in *The Mind of the South*, a book that reads like an exposé of antebellum southern pretension. After all, Cash points out, even without the body of evidence against such claims of aristocratic lineage, it should seem obvious that men of position and power in the Old World would not "embark on frail ships for a dismal frontier where savages prowl and slay."[9] Rather, those willing to undertake such a risk would be laborers facing starvation, debtors anxious to escape jail, or peasants desiring new possibilities. One might think of *Gone with the Wind*, in which Scarlet O'Hara's father, Gerald, an Irish rogue, cleared the trees and built Tara out of nothing, and who earnestly, adamantly compels Scarlet to hold onto the land no matter what happens. He is not a civilized aristocrat from the halls of privilege but an up-by-your-bootstraps frontiersman who affected the manners of a European squire. The fictional Gerald O'Hara follows the actual, historical profile of the first American Percy, Charles Percy.

Although Charles, or "Don Carlos," attempted to leave his history in England, his past caught up with him when his son Robert arrived and revealed to the local community that his father was a bigamist who had abandoned his mother to seek adventure in the New World. Even though Charles had deserted him, Robert sought a relationship with his father, who, at this time, would have been nearing ninety years old. He staked no claims on Charles's large estate—approximately five thousand acres—which would be inherited by his half-brother Thomas Percy, born in America to Charles's second wife. Thus, there are two lines of Percys; Walker was descended from the American set. If you visit St. Francisville today, there are still scores of Percy inhabitants from both lines and even a shared gravestone for Charles and his son Robert in the cemetery of Grace Episcopal Church. In the twentieth-century-poet William Alexander Percy's version of the story, this dramatic return of Charles's first family (which in his unhistorical account included the first wife) drove the founding Percy to despair.

Whether Will Percy's version is true or not, in 1794 this ancestor died by his own hand, a decision that would haunt the rest of his descendants. Tying a tin kettle to his neck, Charles drowned himself in a local creek. There was no recorded motive for his suicide, other than a defeat by melancholia. Of Charles Percy, Will Percy writes, "He was not exactly a credit to anybody, but, as ancestors go, he had his points."[10] One of the points was to amass a small fortune, which would be passed on continually to subsequent Percys. This first Percy made a home in the South and set a precedent of wealth, power, and influence, at least locally. Unfortunately, he also started a trend of suicide, being the first but not the last Percy to take his own life.[11]

Thomas George Percy, Charles's son from his second marriage, married Maria Pope, daughter of LeRoy Pope (notable for their kinship with the British poet Alexander Pope), and moved to Huntsville, Alabama. With the help of four sons, they established a large cotton plantation. Their first son was Walker's original namesake—John Walker—which is also the name of one of Walker Percy's grandsons—and their youngest son was William Alexander, the namesake of Walker's adoptive father. Maria's sister was married to John Williams Walker, whose son LeRoy Pope Walker was the first Confederate secretary of war. In addition to these prestigious figures, the Percys were lawyers, judges, doctors, soldiers, senators, and of course, not to be forgotten—occasionally writers. They held great sway in their region and expected as much from each successive generation.

Walker Percy was born May 28, 1916, in Birmingham, Alabama, the "Magic City," so called for its great industry boom in iron and steel pro-

Introduction: A Brief Biography

duction, not to mention railroads, between 1881 and 1920, all facets of which can be linked to the Percy clan. Walker's father, LeRoy Pratt Percy, was a successful attorney, serving as the general counsel for Tennessee Coal, Iron and Railroad Company, as had his father before him. Elected president of the local country club, LeRoy Percy stood out as a leading figure in the community. Walker's mother, Mattie Sue Phinizy Percy, had been the belle of Athens, Georgia; she was the daughter of the business tycoon Billups Phinizy, heir to the banking fortune amassed by Ferdinand Phinizy. Thus, from both sides, privilege rained down on Walker. Between 1917 and 1922, his parents had two more sons, LeRoy and Phinizy (Phin), whose names continue the show of Percy family pride and consequently baffle biographers' attempts to keep straight the innumerable Walkers, LeRoys, and Phinizys (not to mention Billups, Bollings, William Alexanders, Pratts, and Popes).

Despite this prodigious beginning, Walker Percy suffered subsequent tragedies that marked the course of his life. When he was not yet a year old, his grandfather and namesake shot himself in the heart with a twelve-gauge shotgun. Only hours before his death, the elder Walker had been dining with his son LeRoy, planning a hunting trip to Greenville, Mississippi. Yet, depression suddenly overtook him. Walker ascended to his room and shot himself. To add horror to misery, his son found the body where it had fallen—in his trunk of sporting implements—and became permanently disturbed by it. The media accounts of the incident were varied, reporting about the death circuitously to avoid discussing whether the fatal shooting was volitional. However, the coroner ruled it a suicide. Following in his father's footsteps in many ways, LeRoy was an attorney, a businessman, and an avid hunter. Unfortunately, he also inherited this fatal temperament.

LeRoy Percy reputedly suffered from bouts of depression, swinging from high to low between morning and evening. In hindsight, Walker Percy diagnosed his father as manic-depressive. The medicine for such chemical imbalances did not exist at the time, nor were the resources of psychiatry readily available or well received. In the South, in the 1920s, reputable leaders in the community would lose all standing if they sought such therapy or counseling. Much of LeRoy Percy's melancholy seemed to stem from the pressure he felt to live up to his Percy name, so any admittance of weakness would have increased this despair. His wife, Mattie Sue, sought help within the family, asking his uncle Senator Percy (also named LeRoy) to step in occasionally and talk some sense into her husband. While such chats had a moderate amount of success, LeRoy grew more and more morose. Troubled by his father's suicide for more than a decade, LeRoy Percy, Walker's father, took his own life with a 20-gauge shotgun on July 9, 1929.

There are innumerable psychological motives that could be assigned to Percy's death, and Walker Percy, young and impressionable at thirteen, set about spending his life discovering why his father did it, and more significantly, making sure it didn't happen to him.[12] The search for a father becomes one of the primary quests of Walker's characters, and the disposition towards suicide reappears in each of his novels. Rather than a morbid preoccupation, the reality of suicide, for Percy, made life a choice. Like the philosophers that he would come to revere, Percy too considered the unexamined life not worth continuing.

In 1929, after her husband's suicide, Walker's mother, Mattie Sue, bravely faced the difficult choices before her. She sold off the Birmingham properties, ensuring that she and the boys had no financial concerns. Yet, this also meant they had no place, no home. She must choose to relocate either to her mother's home in Athens or to move in with her husband's cousin William Alexander Percy, a confirmed bachelor in Greenville. Although Mattie Sue hardly knew Will, his parents had been supportive of her and LeRoy during his trials with mental instability. Both LeRoy and his wife Camille had died in the same year as LeRoy—from natural causes—and this grief bonded Mattie Sue with Will. Mattie Sue considered that, if she returned home to Athens permanently, the boys would be surrounded by women, their grandmother and nearby aunts, whereas in Greenville, they would have a male role model.

One could imagine how the young boys interpreted this choice. On the one hand, there was the Billups Phinizy home on the corner of Waddell and Milledge Avenue, with its grand parlor, brass chandeliers, and rosewood furniture. The place was decorated like an Edwardian hotel,

Introduction: A Brief Biography

hosted the appropriate gatherings of southern elites, and its residents required a stern legalistic coherence to Presbyterian values. On the other hand, Will Percy's plantation was filled with souvenirs from his various travels: Moroccan rugs, Japanese paintings, old mahogany furniture, an attic filled with alluring items such as spiked German helmets and bayonets, and an elevator (a source of unending joy for three teenage boys!). Not to mention, Uncle Will's home brought in houseguests the likes of William Faulkner, Langston Hughes, and the Fugitive poets.

Will Percy's invitation to Mattie Sue and the boys must have struck many as overly generous. Why would an isolated bachelor, world traveler, and famous poet alter every aspect of his life by opening up his world to three teenage boys (or nearly teen in Phin's case)? Walker's younger brother LeRoy understood it as an outpouring of the Percy dedication to *noblesse oblige*. It is true that Will Percy never walked away from responsibility. In the famous Great Flood of 1927, he led the Washington County Relief Committee, which rescued thousands from the damaging waters. Only when Will Percy tried to evacuate the Negroes who had been made homeless by the flood was Will Percy forced to step down from his post; the white constituents of his father, Senator LeRoy Percy, were outraged that he would attempt to relocate their primary laborers. From Will's perspective, he was attempting to do what was right for the displaced Negroes. But, to the local planters, he was trying to send away their workforce. He was defeated. Yet, the story is a testament to Will's character, as are many other tales of heroism. The word "duty" or the sense of noblesse oblige does not fully encompass the reasons for Will's actions with regard to the young Percys.

Occupationally, Will Percy was a lawyer-planter, a graduate of Harvard Law, and the inheritor of his father's estate at Trail Lake; but vocationally, he was a poet, which, for Walker in particular, added to his allure and mystique. Before the Percy boys entered his life, he had published a handful of poetry collections, not widely acclaimed but well respected in the literary world. In addition to celebrating Shakespeare and the Romantic poets by reading the works aloud to his new charges, Will Percy would fill the home with classical music, including Stravinsky and Brahms. Walker recalls the heightened excitement his cousin would display when listening to beautiful symphonies and concertos. Moreover, Uncle Will engaged his young charges with tales of his service in World War I. Will would deliver his stories as though he were a knight regaling a court of the recent crusade. Like the inversion of Mark Twain's Connecticut Yankee in King Arthur's Court, Will Percy was a man born in the wrong time.

When William Faulkner reviewed Will Percy's poetry, he accused him of being anachronistic in the modern world. In his poetry and correspondence, Will Percy longs for a time that may have never existed, an idealized South where knights exhibit chivalry and maidens keep their virtue. As an example of his historic archaism, in the fall of 1930, the first year that the Percy boys lived with their uncle, he commissioned a statue to memorialize his father, LeRoy Percy, which emblematizes Percy's view of Stoic virtues, noblesse oblige, and the inherited sense that the Percys are defeated knights among peasantry. Entitled "The Patriot," the statue is a life-size bronze knight with a face reminiscent of LeRoy Percy.[13] He stands in full armor, hands resting on his sword, as he looks downward. The wall behind him is inscribed with the poem "The Last Word" by Matthew Arnold and reads like a Percy manifesto:

> They out talked thee, hissed thee, tore thee
> Better men fared thus before thee. . . .
> Charge once more then and be dumb
> Let the victors when they come
> When the forts of folly fall
> Find thy body by the wall.

Will Percy viewed the modern world as "forts of folly" against which he and his ancestors would fight. He saw the approaching times as "the threshold of chaos" and felt the duty of raising up young knights to confront it. The image of the knight becomes significant for Walker Percy but for different reasons than those of his cousin. While Will Percy charged on behalf of Marcus Aurelius, Walker Percy would choose to follow the knight of faith.[14]

Introduction: A Brief Biography

Within a few months in Will's home, the Percy boys acclimated. They adjusted to their new life, new rooms, new school, and new friends. However, their mother was less fortunate. Although raised with the Victorian ethic of the stiff upper lip, Mattie Sue could not find her place in either Greenville or Trail Lake Plantation. Walker recalls her as distant and mournful in the years after his father's death. One Saturday afternoon, in April 1932, Mattie Sue headed out in her Buick coupe with her son Phin in the backseat. She had no pronounced destination. Suddenly, she drove off a bridge into Deer Creek and was submerged in minutes. Wet and frantic, her son escaped the vehicle and sought help from an oncoming car. Although paramedics dragged her body from the wreck and performed CPR, Mattie Sue was dead when they found her. Whether she suffered heart failure or intentionally crashed the car that day is unknown. From Walker's perspective, she abandoned her sons. He would always recall her accident as one more instance of suicide in the family.

Uncle Will again stepped up and supplied the parent that the boys needed. At forty-five years old, Will Percy adopted all three as the sons he never had. In his memoir, *Lanterns on the Levee*, Will Percy recalls the responsibility of caring for these young men: "I knew a reciprocal duty rested on me to direct them toward the good life in so far as I had discovered it."[15] As much as he could, Uncle Will endeavored to show the three boys the good life. Walker Percy's adoration for and debt to his uncle has been well chronicled. It is from Will Percy that Walker first observed the life of a moralist—as he too would later become—someone who knew his ideals and consciously adhered to them, creating a case study out of his own life to prove the truth about his beliefs. Although Will shared the Romanticism of Walker's father, it was tempered by his Stoicism. For Will, one must triumph over despair. Acting virtuously and doing what was right were more important than being swayed by one's emotions. In Walker Percy's first novel, *The Moviegoer*, he reincarnates his uncle in the character of Aunt Emily.

In addition to high ideals and southern values, Will Percy gifted Walker with his love of literature. Walker suffered from chronic hay fever and was prone to sickness, so he spent much of his time indoors reading from his cousin's vast collection of classic books. Unlike his classmates, who struggled with verse, poetry came easily to Walker, so he sold sonnets for class assignments and published sporadically for the school paper, *The Pica*. His closest friend, Shelby Foote, was later made editor of the publication, and the two shared a lifelong dedication to writing. On trips to the Percys' vacation home at Brinkwood, Tennessee (near Lost Cove Cave, which makes an appearance in *Love in the Ruins*, *The Second Coming*, and *Lost in the Cosmos*), Foote and Percy would hole up like monks and pore over the classics.[16] How many teenage boys today read *War and Peace* and debate with their friends over the merits of Edgar Allan Poe's poetic meter? The two were lucky to have found each other, though luck had little to do with it. Foote had been invited by Will Percy to be a suitable companion for his nephew. When Percy graduated Greenville High School in 1933, he was already far beyond the majority of his peers in literary achievement.

Instead of following the southern tradition, however, and memorizing *Ivanhoe* or *The Adventures of Huckleberry Finn*, Walker became increasingly drawn to scientific narratives, the stories of H. G. Wells and Sinclair Lewis—not that he did not love *Gone with the Wind* and *The Sound and the Fury*, two southern novels that he revered even years later. While Uncle Will had recommended the University of North Carolina at Chapel Hill for its fine English Department, Walker chose to major in the sciences and pursue a career in medicine. He claims Lewis's *Arrowsmith* was the dominant influence on his choice of major. A doctor was one of the choice occupations for a Percy—the others being lawyer, planter, and soldier. Walker describes himself at this juncture as a young Ivan Karamazov seeking to answer the problems of the world with empirical research. Texts such as Huxley's *The Science of Life* excited him with its optimism about human evolution and perpetual progress.

During his college years, Percy dedicated his faith to science. He was certain that the more he learned about the human body, the more he would understand human beings. More significantly, Walker determined to find a cure for himself, for all the anxieties, despair, and memories that haunted him. Science seemed the most probable method for such a discovery. Following graduation, Walker continued his scientific studies at Columbia University, where he received his MD. He specialized in pathology, with an interest in psychiatry placing a close second. During his time in New York, Walker even underwent psychoanalysis under the guidance of Dr. Janet Rioch, an experience he relives through the character of Will Barrett in his second novel, *The Last Gentleman*. His trust in science to diagnose and treat his problems was complete.

However, this trust was soon to prove misplaced. In 1942, while working with cadavers at Bellevue Hospital, Percy contracted tuberculosis. The sickness caused him little pain, but it was a major inconvenience. Percy was forced to uproot his whole life, leave his profession, and retreat to the mountains to recover. At that time, resting in a sanatorium was the only recommended treatment, so Percy checked himself in to the Trudeau Sanatorium located atop a plateau in the Adirondack Mountains. The Edenic setting is near Saranac Lake and is surrounded by giant green trees that point like arrows perpetually upward. Without our current antibiotics, doctors then prescribed seven to ten hours outdoors in a supine position, which meant that Percy spent most of the next few years sleeping, reading, and listening to his radio to receive updates about the war that had recently begun. Both of Percy's brothers enlisted in the service, of which Percy was very jealous. Because patients often exhibited unaccountable weight loss (with Walker and his slight figure surely being no exception), nurses would bring patients, in addition to their three meals, six glasses of milk and six raw eggs a day. On the other side of the world from him, Walker's brothers were fighting a war against the Germans and the Japanese, and there was Percy, sleeping outside and counting calories.

Except for missing the action overseas, Percy spoke of his time at Trudeau as salvific, not only for his health but also for his life. In hindsight, he recalls, "I was the happiest man ever to contract tuberculosis, because it enabled me to get out of Bellevue and quit medicine."[17] Only when free from the path set before him could Percy adequately examine the trajectory of his life and ask the big questions, such as, *What is the meaning of life? Is there a God? Why do humans suffer?* Although Percy credits this time as restorative, in the midst of it he was lonely, isolated, and morose. When removed from the distractions of his studies, his usual penchant for pessimism worsened, and he had very little interaction with the outside world. Foote visited him once and thought him pale and gaunt but content looking. He remembers Percy holding onto his books as though for dear life.[18] Other than Foote and a few amenable residents, Percy kept company with the works of Dostoevsky, Sartre, Kafka, and Mann.

The Mellon Library at Trudeau held between seven thousand and eight thousand titles, and Percy made extensive use of them. While other residents contended for the latest Raymond Chandler detective story, Percy preferred *Notes from the Underground* and *Nausea*. He began to view his stay at Trudeau as an exile, a time of not only physical but also spiritual sickness. For Percy, these books were diagnosing him as much as they were modernity. What he first recognized was that his former method of searching—the scientific method—was limited. Percy writes, "[M]odern science is itself radically incoherent, not when it seeks to understand things . . . but when it seeks to understand man."[19] As opposed to science's empirical limits, novels exhibited the mystery of the thing—the how, the why, and most significantly for Percy, the who. Only in novels did he discover what it meant to be a human being. After returning to New York for a brief stint, Percy's lesion re-flared and, once again, he was confined, this time at a sanatorium in Connecticut, where he slept in the bed of former patient Eugene O'Neill, the Pulitzer Prize–winning playwright and Nobel laureate. His destiny had changed: by becoming a patient, Dr. Percy had decided never to return to medicine. From this time forward, he had a new vocation—to write novels. "But how to go about it?" he would ask himself; and what would he write about?[20]

The war ended nearly simultaneously with Walker's recovery. His Uncle Will had passed away from malignant hypertension only a month after the Japanese bombed Pearl Harbor. His brothers returned home as decorated veterans; LeRoy took over the family plantation in Will's stead. Walker decided to return there as well, not knowing where else to go. After dawdling in Greenville for a bit and feeling full of possibilities but empty of direction, he and Shelby took out on Route 66 to Santa Fe, New Mexico. Neither had plans nor purpose. In Walker's novels, Santa Fe embodies the feelings he had at the time—driftlessness accompanied by a nagging potential. Just as the land itself seemed a beautiful but blank slate, so Percy felt in New Mexico like a new piece of paper upon which the greatest sonnets could be scribed. While relaxing in Santa Fe—or rather, hiding from life, Percy made two substantial decisions quite abruptly: he was going to become a writer and marry Bunt Townsend.

A few years prior to this decision, after Walker finished medical school but before he began his internship at Bellevue, he had volunteered at Gamble Brothers & Archer Clinic in Greenville, where he had met a pathology student, Mary Bernice "Bunt" Townsend. The two became close friends, and Walker kept in touch with her long-distance while in New York and throughout his time at the sanatorium. Although Walker wanted to pursue her, he assumed she found someone else while he was away for so long. Yet, upon making his resolution to marry her, he sent her a hasty letter from Santa Fe informing her to begin planning for their wedding. As Bunt recollects, she was not sure they were getting married until the day of the wedding. But, on November 6, 1946, the two were married in First Baptist Church in New Orleans, the city where Bunt was a student. New Orleans was to become their new home.

That first year of marriage included another significant change for both of them when Walker and Bunt decided to join the Catholic Church. They began taking instructions at Holy Name Church under Father John J. McCarthy and were baptized and confirmed the following Easter Sunday, March 28, 1948. Shelby disdained Walker's decision, calling it "intellectual retreat."[21] However, Walker had been inclining in that direction since his undergraduate days when he roomed with a Catholic schoolmate, Harry Stoval.[22] Percy was impressed with the young man's dedication to attend mass in spite of all the frivolity surrounding him. While in medical school, he encountered Frank Hardart, another devout Catholic, who lived across the hall from him. And, when living at Trudeau, another resident and Roman Catholic, Art Fortugno, introduced him to the work of Thomas Aquinas, which Percy found intellectually satisfying as well as spiritually intriguing. Also, at Fortugno's invitation while at Trudeau, Walker attended mass for the first time. His road to Rome seemed paved.

All of these people, in addition to reading Aquinas and the existentialists, led Percy toward the Catholic Church. Although Percy typically remained close-lipped about his conversion, he answers the question "Why are you a Catholic?" in an essay so titled, written the year he died and posthumously published. His summary thesis is, "The reason I am a Catholic is that I believe that what the Catholic Church proposes is true."[23] For Percy, the truth of the Gospels was authoritative and not up for debate. His intellectual assent to this claim followed from his reading of an essay by Søren Kierkegaard, which was to be the catalyst for his conversion. Kierkegaard's essay "Of the Difference Between a Genius and an Apostle" convinced Percy that the messages of apostles were authoritative in a way that the writings of novelists and other such thinkers were not. While the genius speaks from his or her own mind, the apostle brings a message from elsewhere, from a transcendent source. Because the apostle speaks on behalf of the divine, what she or he says has authority. Once Percy recognized the Gospels as dictated by apostles and not mere geniuses, the only option was to assent or disregard the authority. He chose the former option and was baptized.

Cradle-Catholic and fellow southern writer Flannery O'Connor once wrote, "All voluntary baptisms are a miracle to me and stop my mouth as much as if I had just seen Lazarus walk out of the tomb."[24] Percy would not have disagreed, and such a statement surely describes his own conversion. As a boy, Walker's father was fascinated by religion, but without all the divine nonsense. He taught Sunday School at their Presbyterian Church, a church whose minister was considered apostate by other congregations for his egregious splicing out of the miraculous bits from the Bible. In a letter to another convert and southern novelist Caroline Gordon, Percy calls his father's library "creepy," comprised of "many religious works, but all of the liberal-scholarly-protestant variety which stemmed from 19th century German rationalism by way of English divines." He calls such reading "lethal to the faith."[25] In contrast to the nominal faith of his father, Walker's adoptive father Will Percy

Introduction: A Brief Biography

was a religious zealot for the Catholic faith until he turned away in his twenties.

Although once determined to become a priest, Will Percy lost his faith while an undergraduate at the University of the South. His father had been a lax Episcopalian and his mother a lukewarm Catholic; Will chose to be an ardent version of the latter. In his first years of school, he would trek ten to fourteen miles down the mountain road to Good Shepherd Catholic Church to make confession and receive the sacrament. Yet, at some indefinable point in his career at Sewanee, Will stopped believing. Most likely, his loss of faith was incited by the accidental death of his younger brother, LeRoy.[26] Whatever the cause, from approximately 1902 forward, Will Percy dissolved his once fervent relationship to the church. Despite his memorable declaration that "no priest could absolve me, no church could direct my life or my judgment," Will still felt a fondness for Catholicism throughout his life.[27] Perhaps this distant reverence for the church somehow seeped into the wakes of Walker's consciousness.

A few years before his death in 1990, Walker Percy summarized the events of his life into four milestones:

> one, losing both parents in my early teens and being adopted by my uncle, a poet, and being exposed to the full force of a remarkable literary imagination; two, contracting a nonfatal case of tuberculosis while serving as an intern in Bellevue Hospital in New York, an event that did not so much change my life as give me leave to change it; three, getting married; four, becoming a Catholic. (*Signposts* 374)

These events sound like a pitch for a strange film, but they are the plot points of Percy's life. Although he lived into his seventies, Percy's four events all occurred before his thirty-third birthday, a significant birthday for Christians for it is the age that Jesus died and completed his ministry. I cannot help pointing out that Percy does not list the titles of his novels nor his awards or sales figures as defining moments of his life. Yet, all four moments made Percy the novelist that he was.

After Percy joined the Roman Catholic Church, his desire to write novels became inextricably linked with his career as a moralist. He felt he discovered how to live a life, and he wanted to encourage others toward this truth. A resounding theme throughout his fiction is the "living-dead." His protagonists often remark that everyone around them seems dead, to be walking around without paying any attention to the world, and to be talking without noticing the meaning of his or her words. To counteract this culture of zombies and the century of the love of death, Percy writes about "what it is to be born a human individual, to live, and to die" (*Signposts* 288). He investigates how in twentieth-century America, where all are needs are met and all the experts are telling us how to have successful lives, we are all so unhappy. Yet, Percy understood his limitations as a novelist, which is why the majority of his novels end ambiguously, with an ellipses or "to be continued" motion. As a novelist, Percy thought he could be a diagnostician, but not the healer.

Percy wrote six novels between 1961 and 1987, and published two essay collections and a humorous work entitled *Lost in the Cosmos* (1983), which has gained quite a cult following. His first novel received the National Book Award, his next two novels received nominations, and his last three novels were popular successes, especially *The Second Coming*, which made bestseller lists. When Walker Percy died in 1990, at seventy-four, he thought himself the "oldest male Percy in history" (*Correspondence* 179). His Catholic faith showed him how to make sure that his father's fate of an early volitional death did not happen to him. It also showed him how to die, as Percy writes in the final months of his life: "Dying, if that's what it comes to, is no big thing since I'm ready for it, and prepared for it by the Catholic faith which I believe" (302). Not only in his fiction but also in his life, Percy explored what it meant to be a human being, to live and to die.

Over a century after Percy's birth and half a century after his first novel, his work has greater relevance to this time than when it was originally published. Recognizing Percy's aptness to the surreal theater of the 2016 American presidential race, bloggers began their analyses of election drama with "Happy Birthday" messages to Percy to celebrate his centennial. Moviegoing is no longer an occasional pastime but a way

Introduction: A Brief Biography

to fill any empty minute by flipping on the Netflix app on your phone. There are no more last gentlemen, and what was laughable about American politics in 1971 has suffocated the metaphorical canary in 2016. *Eros* is not defeating *thanatos*, for the twenty-first century has already shown itself as capable of violence as the twentieth century of terror. All that to say that we are more lost in the cosmos than ever before. What we need are more readers of Walker Percy.

In 2011, I joined a group of Percy aficionados on a short pilgrimage to the novelist's gravesite at St. Joseph Abbey in Covington, Louisiana. We wanted to pay our respects to a man most of us had never met but by whom we nonetheless felt intimately known. We had spent a weekend expounding upon Percy's ideas, reading conference papers on his novels to one another, and in the evening, in true Percy fashion, toasting our literary saint with clinking glasses of bourbon on balconies lining St. Charles Avenue. Then, around 10:00 on Saturday morning, when most of New Orleans is either in deep muggy sleep or else blowing powdered sugar off fresh beignets, a dozen of us loaded into a white bus to cross the Causeway Bridge over Lake Pontchartrain, toward his grave. Like Grace Episcopal Church, where the first Percy in America is memorialized, St. Joseph Abbey is a beautiful nineteenth-century red-brick building with high arches and stained-glass windows. The grounds are far-reaching and green, with hundred-year-old trees spread out as though, for these monks, God planted sanctuaries from the heat under which to pray. We stood near one tree beside which was the small, unadorned plaque marking Percy's grave. As we stood quietly around the stone, one woman began singing "Ave Maria." A car pulled up, and Percy's widow, Bunt, stepped out, aided by her daughter Anne. I glanced down at the plaque, which read, "Walker Percy, May 28, 1916–May 10, 1990," and I thought of Shelby Foote's final words memorializing his friend: "I would state my hope that Walker Percy will be seen in time for what he was in simple and solemn fact—a novelist [. . .]. [His subject]—and all the rest of ours, for that matter—was the same: 'the human heart in conflict with itself'" (*Correspondence* 304). That subject, like the work of Percy, is timeless.

1
The Moviegoer

When you wake up, brew your coffee, pack your pockets with keys, wallet, cell phone, and walk out the door, do you ever wonder: What is the point of it all? There's traffic to contend with, telemarketers to shoo away, bills to haggle, and the day-to-day monotony of work, eat, play. How to escape the tedium of life, the ennui of existence? As Binx Bolling, the existential hero of Walker Percy's first novel, *The Moviegoer* (1961), approaches his thirtieth birthday, these questions begin to gnaw at him. At the start of the novel, John Bickerson (Binx) Bolling is a lost man. As a stockbroker who works for his uncle, Binx spends his free time wandering the streets of New Orleans, dallying with secretaries on the weekends, and going to the movies as often as possible to avoid the boredom and isolation of everydayness. The week before his thirtieth birthday, however, Binx initiates a search for the meaning of life. By the end of the novel, his search seems to have led him onto a path with a definite destination.

When readers first meet Binx, he is a typical American businessman, a young bachelor "living the most ordinary life imaginable" (9). In one sentence, he summarizes his life: "I am a model tenant and a model citizen and take pleasure in doing all that is expected of me" (6). He sounds much like W. H. Auden's "The Unknown Citizen": "He was found by the Bureau of Statistics to be / One against whom there was no official complaint."[1] As evidence of his "model" citizenry, Binx collects identity cards, library cards, and credit cards. He lists for the reader his observance of consumer practices, his obedience to the wisdom of the experts on everything from mental health to safe driving and his belief in the authority of celebrities: "I subscribe to *Consumer Reports* and as a consequence I own a first-class television set, an all but silent air conditioner and a very long lasting deodorant. My armpits never stink" (*MG*

7). Percy's irony is subtle, but Binx suppresses any discontent by consuming products and fulfilling his societal obligations. He calls this the "Little Way, not the big search for the big happiness but the sad little happiness of drinks and kisses, a good little car and a warm deep thigh" (135–36). He is Voltaire's Candide cultivating his own garden, or Dostoevsky's Underground Man hiding in a suburban basement or the dark of a movie theater. He is the Everyman who strives against inconvenience and is seemingly content with middle-class privilege. The inciting incident for Binx's transformation is a recollection of what he calls "the search": "The search is what anyone would undertake if he were not sunk in the everydayness of his own life. . . . To become aware of the possibility of the search is to be on to something. Not to be onto something is to be in despair" (13).

Everydayness is the humdrum banality of ordinary existence—laundry, dentist appointments, or that perpetual grocery list on the fridge.[2] It is our way of being in the world without reflection. Binx describes the search in opposition to "despair," to living apathetically and inattentively. He refers to the epigraph of the novel from Søren Kierkegaard's *The Sickness Unto Death*: "[T]he specific character of despair is precisely this: it is unaware of being despair."[3] One lives in despair when one is "no more aware of the mystery which surrounds him than a fish is aware of the water it swims in" (*MG* 52); it is a mindless, careless, routeless existence.

Binx does not define the end of the search. Rather ironically, he mentions God as a possible objective: "What do you seek—God? You ask with a smile" (13). He admits that the concept of God is challenging to him: "I have only to hear the word God and a curtain comes down in my head" (145). Although Binx was raised in a Catholic home, it has made little difference to him. He insists that God himself could appear, and nothing would change. Another possibility for the end of the search is the "big happiness." By this, Binx means what philosophers like Aristotle or Thomas Aquinas would call the *summum bonum* or the highest good in life, in contrast to the little happiness, which can be purchased, consumed, and wasted. Rather than a temporary and fleeting happiness, Binx seeks an unchanging happiness that will overcome his everyday despair. Like the vague "Answer to the Ultimate Question of Life, the Universe, and Everything" that is sought in *The Hitchhiker's Guide to the Galaxy*, Binx's search is a quest to discover what makes life worth living.

One can hear echoes of the American tradition in his thoughts. In the previous century, the American transcendentalist Henry David Thoreau yells, "Wake up!" to those around him whom he saw as sleepwalkers merely dancing through life without engaging. Similarly, Binx imagines others as walking dead. When engaging in small talk with other people, Binx thinks, "this is death" (100). Only a decade before him, Ralph Ellison had depicted the "living death" in the form of his zombie-like protagonist in *Invisible Man*. And twenty-first-century filmmakers and TV producers have capitalized on this observation with *Shaun of the Dead* (2004), *Warm Bodies* (2013), and *The Walking Dead* (2010–present) in which humans have relinquished their humanity and become literally the living dead. Thoreau's sleepwalkers are today's zombies. But Binx wants more, and he thinks the search offers the answer.

The possibility of the search is instigated by Binx's pile of belongings on his bureau. He awakes one morning and sees them for the first time as though they belonged to someone else. "They looked both unfamiliar and at the same time full of clues," he remarks (*MG* 11). While previously Binx had been living without paying conscious attention to his life, the sight of his belongings returns him to the search. "Once I saw it," Binx notes, "the search became possible" (11). Attending to the objects before him extracts Binx from everydayness and puts him on the search. The search first occurred to Binx several years before when he found himself in a fix while serving in the Korean War. Waking in a ditch, bleeding beneath a chindolea bush with a dung beetle no more than six inches from his nose, Binx promises himself to pursue the search. Yet, when he returns home safe and sound, he forgets all about his promise. Instead Binx settles into the suburbs of Gentilly, goes to work each day for his uncle, and watches movies—a card-carrying member of the living dead. What recalls the search to his mind, however, is the pile of belongings sitting atop his bureau. Seeing his identify objectified—literally, reduced to objects—Binx feels unsatisfied for the first time in a long while. This moment of attentiveness and subsequent self-reflection stirs something deeper in him.

In this recollection, Binx implies that the closeness of death inspires the search. This theme reoccurs several times in the novel. By the end of the first page, Binx recalls the death of his older brother, Scotty. His father's death also acts as a clue in the search, as does the death of his cousin's fiancé, Lyell, and finally the death of his half-brother, Lonnie, at the conclusion of the novel. When his cousin Kate survives the same car crash that kills her fiancé, she discovers how death propels one out of everydayness. Walking away from the accident, she rides a bus to a hotel, and it is the "happiest moment" of her life: "the door opened, then I got on and we went sailing along from bright sunshine down through deep clefts as cool and dark as a spring house" (58). The nearness of death compels her to prize her own existence. However, without the constant reminder that life is a choice, Kate is scared into stasis. In contrast, Binx, who has been living thoughtlessly, becomes derailed by the inevitability of death. It causes him to register discontent with his carelessly happy existence. Aleksandr Solzhenitsyn once said, "[If] man is born to be happy, he would not be born to die."[4] By recognizing their mortality, Binx and Kate feel freed from the transitory and insufficient happiness offered in this life. Instead, they desire something more from their life, something like the big happiness, something eternal.

The search has made Binx aware of his existential dilemma, his alienation from his self, his world, and the God in which he does not believe. What he dreads from everydayness is the impending *malaise*, which he defines as "the pain of loss": "The world is lost to you, the world and the people in it, and there remains only you and the world and you no more able to be in the world than Banquo's ghost" (120).[5] If one surrenders to the malaise, which is symptomatic of everydayness, he or she may become "No One Nowhere" (99). But how does this happen? What does Binx mean that we may become "No One Nowhere"?

For Percy, this is a modern problem facing most individuals in his culture, but the roots begin with a seventeenth-century philosophical shift initiated by René Descartes. In *Meditations on First Philosophy*, Descartes—in his attempt to prove the existence of God—questions his knowledge of everything, talking himself out of all knowledge except *Cogito ergo sum* or "I think, therefore I am." Thus, Descartes begins his project by locating the self in the mind, and it is this capacity to think that grants him existence. This famous assertion is responsible for the "Cartesian split," the divide of the self into body and mind, and the subsequent division of the world into concrete, empirical reality versus abstract ideas. In his 1980 nonfiction work *Lost in the Cosmos*, Percy blames the French Enlightenment thinker for the beginning of the confusion:

> The Self since the time of Descartes has been stranded, split off from everything else in the Cosmos, a mind which professes to understand bodies and galaxies but is by the very act of understanding marooned in the Cosmos, with which it has no connection. It therefore needs to exercise every option in order to reassure itself that it is not a ghost but is rather a self among other selves. (44)

Like Binx in his reference to Banquo's ghost, Percy emphasizes the wraith-like existence of one who is isolated, alienated, and split asunder into flesh and mind.

Binx first discovers this predicament one summer when he and a classmate are conducting research at the university. While working in the lab studying the formation of renal calculi in pigs—a subtle joke by Percy—Binx becomes affected by the way the sunlight falls in yellow bars across the room. He listens to the creaking of the old building and the students outside playing touch football and becomes dismissive of his research. In contrast, his lab partner Harry Stern remains oblivious. He was "unaffected by the singularities of time and place": "His abode was anywhere. It was all the same to him whether he catheterized a pig at four o'clock in the afternoon in New Orleans or at midnight in Transylvania" (*MG* 52). Focused on the scientific problem at hand, Harry rises above the particularities of his empirical world while Binx begins to register this transcendence as a quandary common to scientists.

In an earlier version of his search, Binx pursued science as part of a "vertical search." He read books such as Schrödinger's *What Is Life?*

and Einstein's *The Universe as I See It*. He notes, "I stood outside the universe and sought to understand it" (69). Later in his 1983 *Lost in the Cosmos*, Percy returns to this problem of the vertical search, calling scientists and artists who undertake this search "transcending selves" because they levitate above the world to solve certain puzzles about the universe, only to return to earth to face the indecipherable mystery of the self. Binx reflects, "The only difficulty [with the vertical search] was that though the universe had been disposed of [that is, learned about and understood], I myself was left over" (70). Although science could explain everything from the temperature of the sun to the code of our DNA, it never could describe the self, what it is that makes Percy himself or Binx, Binx. Percy writes about this discovery: "[T]he more science progressed, and even as it benefited man, the less it said about what it is like to be a man living in the world" (*Signposts* 188). From its vantage point, science looks down upon the human being and makes it an organism in an environment, a specimen beneath a microscope. Percy warns against this stance: "[I]t is little help to us scientifically to regard man as a composite of body, mind, and soul, and that it is a positive hindrance if we think this explains anything" (114). Science cannot help recover a right understanding of what it means to be a self in the world.

The Moviegoer attempts the small feat of reunifying these pieces. In his acceptance speech for the National Book Award, Percy summarizes his goal for *The Moviegoer*: "In short, the book attempts a modest restatement of the Judeo-Christian notion that man is more than an organism in an environment, more than an integrated personality, more even than a mature and creative individual, as the phrase goes. He is a wayfarer and a pilgrim" (*Signposts* 246). While Percy feared that his book did not succeed, many readers at least acknowledge the authenticity of Binx's search. Binx begins as a moviegoer and ends—though it is not an *ending* at all—as a wayfarer.

As a moviegoer, Binx uses movies as a short-term solution to his alienation, while also recognizing movies as part of the problem. Because movies mediate reality for him, they perpetuate his sense of Cartesian dualism and allow him to live like an actor apart from himself.

Over the course of the novel, Binx references a dozen movies, thirty-seven actors, and eight actresses.[6] He views his situation in terms of a movie, posturing himself at a distance from the world, ready to act in any given situation as others expect of him. Towards the end of the book, Binx encounters another moviegoer, whom he also calls the "romantic" (a moniker that refers back to Binx's father).[7] The romantic does not go to movies but, like Binx's father, needs books to supply meaning to the mundane activities of his day. However, the romantics are as disappointed as the moviegoers because the real never lives up to the idealized version of lived experience. For instance, near the start of the novel, Binx eyes a girl on a bus. While they awkwardly glance at one another, Binx fails to introduce himself, and the two separate at their disparate stops. However, if it were a movie, the scene would play out differently. The hero and his damsel would be thrown together by a bus crash, and the life-or-death scenario would heighten all their senses. In the passion of the moment, the man and woman would fall into each other's arms. This gap between the ideal world of the movies and reality resurfaces at the climax of the novel when Binx and Kate travel to Chicago.

Another way that movies mediate reality is by "certifying" particular places. After watching the movie *Panic in the Streets*, Kate observes that their neighborhood, which was featured in the movie, has now been certified. Binx explains: "Nowadays when a person lives somewhere, in a neighborhood, the place is not certified for him. [. . .] But if he sees a movie which shows his very neighborhood, it becomes possible for him to live, for a time at least, as a person who is Somewhere and not Anywhere" (*MG* 63). Binx refers to the problem of placelessness, another consequence of Descartes's meditations. The world suffers a hangover from Descartes's attempt to make us all into free-floating minds. Aware of the tendency toward dislocation and disembodiment, Binx prefers to stay situated in New Orleans, a place that has been certified for him.

Add to all of these perks from moviegoing two more, "rotation" and "repetition," which Binx cites explicitly. Percy borrows these terms from the existentialists that he loved (namely Kierkegaard),[8] but Binx offers his own definitions. "A rotation," he says, is "the experience of the new beyond the experiencing of the new" (*MG* 144). Percy clarifies this definition more fully in his 1956 essay "The Man on the Train." Rotation is Huck Finn traveling the Mississippi River and experiencing new adventures around each bend, or Don Quixote on his ever-continuous quest for escapade after escapade. We may seek rotation by traveling to foreign places or vicariously through the drama of a televised soap opera, or, as Binx does, in movies. Those absorbed by everydayness use rotations as a poor means of escape from feeling bored with their lives. In movies, characters don't stand in line at the DMV on a Wednesday afternoon. Instead, Gary Cooper stands alone in a dusty street and guns down his enemies. Every scene in a movie is extraordinary. Movies are "onto the search," as Binx says. However, "they screw it up" (*MG* 13). Although the action and unexpected events provide rotation, they end happily ever after. Even if they end unhappily, the movies wrap up in a neat and tidy way. Binx laments how often the castaway and his heroine fall in love, marry, and move to suburbia. While the hero may have started a path out of everydayness, he ends "so sunk in everydayness that he might just as well be dead" (13). When the curtain closes on *Spellbound*, for instance, the viewer imagines Gregory Peck and Ingrid Bergman will spend the rest of their evenings eating lasagna and discussing whether to paint the walls pea green or sea foam. In movies, the search "always ends in despair" (13).

Another method of escape that movies provide is repetition. According to Binx, "A repetition is the re-enactment of past experience toward the end of isolating the time segment which has lapsed in order that it, the lapsed time, can be savored of itself and without the usual adulteration of events that clog the time like peanuts in brittle" (79–80). The days run together as we get up each morning, go to work, eat breakfast lunch and dinner, kiss our kids goodnight, make love with our spouses, say our prayers, dream of other worlds, and wake again to live the same day. How then do we locate ourselves in this story in which our memories cloud together like a surrealist or impressionist painting with Thursday last week looking no different from Wednesday this week? Repetitions pull out these memories and make them concrete and tangible once again. By revisiting the place or reenacting a moment, we locate ourselves in the world again. For example, Binx escorts his new secretary, Sharon, on the same journey to the beach and to his mother's vacation home that he has once shared with his previous secretaries, Marcia and Linda—repetition and rotation.

In addition to moviegoing, Binx discovers, as does his second cousin, Kate, that disaster may break one out of the malaise. After surviving a deadly car crash, Kate realizes that death freed her from despair. She is so happy to be alive. However, the pain of a seemingly pointless existence continues to return. She questions Binx: "Have you noticed that only in time of illness or disaster or death are people real?" (81). Kate uses drugs, attempts suicide, and picks at her fingers until they bleed. She chases pain as a way of escaping the malaise. Binx recognizes the positive effects of disaster when he endures a minor car crash. When Sharon and Binx are cruising towards the beach in his MG, he feels the malaise begin to settle in. Then, they are sideswiped by some tourists, and the day is redeemed. The malaise has been cast off by a brush with death. Critics call this Percy's "hurricane theory," his idea that people feel better in bad environments, like a sudden hurricane, than in good environments. Binx reflects, "Perhaps there was a time when everydayness was not too strong and one could break its grip by brute strength. Now nothing breaks it—but disaster" (145). While moviegoing and disasters break one from everydayness, neither are long-lasting solutions. In part, the bond between Kate and Binx stems from their mutual recognition of the malaise and their search for a permanent escape from despair.

Surrounding Binx and Kate are people unknowingly in despair, who feel satisfied with how they have defined their life purpose. For Percy, this move to autonomous self-determination is one of the primary problems of modern society. In the twentieth century and continuing in this millennium, there is no longer a general assumption about how to view the world and one's role in it.[9] In place of Judeo-Christian beliefs, American ideals of hard work and doing the right thing, or even the southern traditions of manners are individual choices about what to believe and how to live. People make up their own meaning of life. A radio program called "This I Believe"—which Binx listens to each night—epitomizes this widespread phenomenon.[10] Each caller composes his or her own creed: "I believe in music. I believe in a child's smile. I believe in love. I also believe in hate" (MG 109). Binx observes, "Everyone on This I Believe believes in the uniqueness of the individual. I have noticed, however, that the believers are far from unique themselves, are in fact alike as peas in a pod" (109). Whereas the universal belief systems of the old variety, such as Judaism and Christianity, were persecuted for inducing conformity, the new method of absolute autonomy actually produces the more programmed adherents. Not wanting to become one of these automatons himself, Binx is frozen, unable to resolve how to carry out his life.

For Binx, the search starts with attention to the objects on his bureau and continues with attention to everything around him, especially to those who surround him with their competing worldviews. Like a scientist collecting specimens, Binx spells out each character's view of life and weighs the options against one another. He begins to develop a scale that lines up with Kierkegaard's famous stages of existence. The nineteenth-century Dane asserted three levels toward true selfhood: the aesthetic, the ethical, and the religious. In the first level, the aesthetic, pleasures are the driving principle. People act according to pleasure and plain, chasing the former and avoiding the latter. There is no self-reflection or rationalization of options, but rather passion moves one towards perceived goods indiscriminate of whether a decision is right or wrong.

For most of *The Moviegoer*, Binx resides in the aesthetic sphere of existence. He has distracted himself from any examination of his life choices with big-bottomed brunettes and plans to purchase a filling station. And he is not alone. The Lovells, for instance, are also aesthetes, the "chief representatives of everydayness."[11] They spend their time redecorating their house, networking, and participating in book clubs for self-improvement. They pursuit the little happiness as the ultimate end, understanding "everything out there and everything out there is something to be understood" (MG 19). Nothing is higher than Lovell judgment, and nothing more is wanted than life with its small distractions.

However, after Binx's discovery of the objects on his bureau, the aesthetic life is no longer possible. Self-reflection is the first step out of the aesthetic level. In his most famous sermon, "The Weight of Glory," C. S. Lewis indicts all people as aesthetes by nature. "We are half-hearted creatures," he laments: "fooling about with drink and sex and ambition when infinite joy is offered us, like an ignorant child who wants to go on making mud pies in a slum because he cannot imagine what is meant by the offer of a holiday at the sea. We are far too easily pleased."[12] Binx is not pleased. He is bored with drink and sex and ambition. He once tried such a life with a couple of war buddies: "We were all pretty good drinkers and talkers and we could spiel about women and poetry and Eastern religion in pretty good style. [. . .] But in no time at all I became depressed" (*MG* 41). He notices that such living distracts one from the "wonder," or what Lewis would call infinite joy.[13] Binx is searching for that. Yet, he does not find the Catholic faith of his relatives initially compelling.

From Binx's perspective, his mother and Uncle Jules do not appear to live examined lives. Although Jules is a Catholic, he's rather nonchalant in regard to the faith. Binx notes, "For the world [Uncle Jules] lives in, the City of Man is so pleasant that the City of God must hold little in store for him" (*MG* 31). He enjoys making money and talking football, and he avoids all conflict either familial or regional. Jules is a resident of the City of Man, and Binx twice calls his mother "Eve." Her faith is "but one of the devices that come to hand in an outrageous man's world" (142). After the death of her son Duval, her Catholic faith has become compartmentalized away from the rest of her life. When Binx attends Mass with his family, he employs the same metaphor when referencing the participants as the one he uses for the tourists crowding the ferry; all are packed like sardines—vacant eyed and nondescript. Because of Binx's invincible unbelief, he sees no difference between those sunk in everydayness and his Catholic relatives, apart from his half-brother Lonnie, who will later have a great effect on Binx's conversion.

The most prominent worldview that Binx observes is preached by Aunt Emily, exemplar extraordinaire of the second of Kierkegaard's modes—the ethical. The ethical mode of being is guided by values. When one's desires conflict with what is deemed good, then the good takes precedence. The passions are reined in. Binx describes Emily as "Episcopalian by emotion, a Greek by nature and a Buddhist by choice" (*MG* 23). She is a veritable cornucopia of worldviews, all of her own choosing, and with one common thread—ethics. Emily embodies Stoicism, an ancient Greek philosophy that promotes virtue for its own sake. In a memo to Binx, Aunt Emily quotes Emperor Marcus Aurelius, who typifies this belief system: "Every moment think steadily as a Roman and a man, to do what thou hast in hand with perfect and simple dignity, and a feeling of affection and freedom and justice" (78).[14] Several times in the narrative, for instance when Binx loses his brother Scotty, Aunt Emily encourages Binx to act like a soldier. Aunt Emily is a bastion of antebellum ideals, including the belief that southern gentlemen live and die by their lights; they are to act like soldiers noble and stalwart even if civilization crumbles around them.

While Binx finds his Aunt's ideals admirable, he does not understand their purpose. Percy comments on Binx's confusion: "He just doesn't believe in being the honorable man, doing the right thing, for its own sake."[15] When Emily lambasts Binx at the conclusion of the novel, he falters in his search and longs to return to his "Little Way" of hedonism and consumption: "My search has been abandoned; it is no match for my aunt, her rightness and her despair" (*MG* 228). Despite his recognition of her "rightness," her way is not only inaccessible to him, it is still one of despair. To Binx, her ethical sphere is as pointless as the bent-sword letter opener that she fidgets with as she lectures him. Indeed, the small sword—whose tip Binx bent years earlier trying to open a drawer—becomes emblematic of the ineffectiveness of her Stoicism.

In his essay on "Stoicism in the South," Percy argues that the problem with southerners' values is that they are more Stoic than Christian. "The South's virtues," Percy writes, "were the broadsword virtues of the clan, as were her vices, too—the hubris of *noblesse* gone arrogant" (*Signposts* 84). For whatever good that noblesse oblige brought out in people—responsibility, honor, duty—it was limited by its fallacious view of human hierarchy. Aunt Emily prides herself on her class; because of her values, she considers herself higher than the common man, especially the black man or the poor man. She confesses to Binx,

"We're better because we do not shirk our obligations either to ourselves or to others" (*MG* 223). Her words echo a similar aristocratic arrogance found in William Alexander Percy's autobiography, *Lanterns on the Levee: Recollections of a Planter's Son*; Will Percy had little tolerance for those he deemed poor whites.[16] Although Walker Percy cautions readers against casting judgment backward on people like his uncle who were products of their time, he does insist that such condescension has no place in the future.[17] Both Will Percy's and Aunt Emily's seemingly noble way falls flat, unable to fulfill Binx's search for an answer.

Instead of "The Little Way" or the "Old Way" of the South, Binx must find the Way, epitomized by the third level in Kierkegaard's system, the religious sphere. Here, actions may or may not make logical sense. All values are drawn from a mysterious transcendent. Kierkegaard explicates the story from the Jewish Torah or Christian Old Testament when Abraham is commanded by God to kill his son Isaac. To do so would be morally reprehensible but religiously sound. This exemplifies a life in the religious level, one that ultimately follows divine law above human law.

In order to make that leap, which Binx does, into the religious sphere, his "Little Way" must fail him. The climax of the novel begins with a train ride to Chicago. When Binx's Uncle Jules asks Binx to visit Chicago for business, Binx sweats and curses over such an assignment because the journey removes him from the particularity of his place and time. It may even rob him of his search (*MG* 98–99). Binx has already expressed his disapproval of traveling to a strange city where he will feel untethered to reality. As he puts it, "[T]he spirit-presence of a strange place can enrich a man or rob a man but never leave him alone" (99). However, the train ride increases his discomfort because of the extended time spent in no place. The passengers are in perpetual motion, but unlike Huck Finn, there is no adventure around the corner. Moreover, the conversations aboard the train are fatal: people engage in small talk, acting out roles with one another. Nothing is authentic.

Stepping off the train into the strange, massive city, Binx longs for someone to tell him the details about the train station, the history of it, and so forth. "Every place of arrival should have a booth set up," Binx proposes, "and manned by an ordinary person whose task it is to greet strangers and give them a little trophy of local space-time stuff in order to insure that the stranger shall not become an Anyone" (202). This fear of being cut loose from space and time drives Binx to familiarize himself with the managers at his local movie theaters, so he can concretize his existence. It is out of fear of the *malaise*, of losing his place in the world, that while in Chicago he ventures off to see his old war-buddy Harold Graebner. He needs a witness who knows him to vouch for his existence in Chicago.

Binx's Cartesian delusions are further confronted by his sexual encounter with Kate aboard the train. He and Kate attempt a night of passion that ends in failure. Feigning a dialogue with the actor Rory Calhoun,[18] Binx grieves, "Flesh poor flesh failed us. The burden was too great and flesh poor flesh, neither hallowed by sacrament nor despised by spirit . . . quails and fails" (200). The physical act demands more from him than he can give. Although Binx lacks the theological vocabulary needed to categorize his dilemma, he feels that something is missing in their encounter. Binx reflects, "Christians talk about the horror of sin, but they have overlooked something. They keep talking as if everyone were a great sinner, when the truth is that nowadays one is hardly up to it" (200). For Binx, this failure, accompanied by the awareness that there must be something more, begins a transformation in him.

There is one final moment where Binx wavers over whether to return to his aesthetic way or to move into the religious. After the failed sexual encounter, Binx returns with Kate early from Chicago because his aunt is infuriated that he took his mentally unstable cousin with him without notifying anyone. She rightly lights into him about this thoughtlessness and selfishness. Although unconvinced by her spiel, it does convince Binx to surrender the search: "My search has been abandoned; it is no match for my aunt's rightness and her despair" (228). Immediately after this dialogue, Binx returns to his hedonistic ways and calls his secretary, Sharon. Thankfully, Kate meets him before he surrenders to the aesthetic stage again. In conversation with her, all of his recent experiences, his collection of data on the search, the trip to Chicago—everything comes together in his mind at the right moment.

The novel began with Binx meeting Aunt Emily and her request to know by his birthday what he planned to do with his life, and by that day, which falls on Ash Wednesday, he has decided. "There is only one thing I can do," Binx concludes, "listen to people, see how they stick themselves into the world, hand them along a ways on their dark journey, and be handed along for good and selfish reasons" (233). Like a child climbing a ladder for the first time, Binx is slowly ascending from his aesthetic level. As he peers out the window at the church across the street, he sees a vision that acts as a catalyst for his future conversion. A Negro man has received the ashes and is now praying over the steering wheel of his Mercury. Witnessing the scene, Binx wonders whether something spiritual as well as empirical has occurred here:

> It is impossible to say why he is here. Is it part and parcel of the complex business of coming up in the world? Or is it because he believes that God himself is present here at the corner of Elysian Fields and Bons Enfants? Or is he here for both reasons: through some dim dazzling trick of grace, coming for the one and receiving the other as God's own importunate bonus? (235)

He concludes, "It is impossible to say." He repeats the phrase three times in emphasis. His once invincible unbelief has been chinked by doubt.

Although Percy had set out to incarnate his newfound Catholic beliefs in fiction, he faltered with how to accomplish such a goal without turning off the reader. His editor, Stanley Kauffmann, advocated for ambiguity. He suggested that Percy refrain from "rather handily" tying up the search at the end, as he had done previously. "One doesn't ask for the unanswerable to be answered," Kauffmann advises.[19] After much dicing and splicing of his original manuscript, the Catholic conversion of Binx is muted and often missed by readers.

In addition to Kauffmann's revisions of the manuscript, Percy took to heart what Kierkegaard had taught him in "Of the Difference between a Genius and an Apostle," which influenced not only Percy's conversion but also his development as a novelist. For the "genius," Kierkegaard argues, the goal is to uncover truth and as an artist put forward an entertaining vision of what one has discovered. The novelist is a genius who does not offer new wisdom, but rather validates through narrative what everyone knows but perhaps has not considered that way before. New geniuses come about in every age, and their wisdom is often nothing new under the sun. In contrast to the genius, the apostle does not *find* truth in experience but receives revelation from outside of oneself. Every word from his or her mouth is authoritative and on the part of another. The knowledge of the apostle is transcendent. Kierkegaard offers the example of Peter and John, uneducated men who impressed the intellectual Jews in the Sanhedrin (Acts 4). When the apostle speaks, people must listen and do as he says. In various interviews and essays, Percy echoed what he learned from Kierkegaard: "[The novelist] doesn't have the authority to be edifying. His vocation has to do with narrative, entertainment, perhaps verification or certification of experience" (*More Conversations* 159). Percy knew that his role was as the former, as a genius, not an apostle.

However, if Percy wanted his fiction to be edifying, even as a "by-product," as he suggests (159), he had to take the "indirect method" (146). Kauffmann recommends wisely that Percy avoid "homily or pabulum" but still give "definition" and conclusion to the question, "[W]hat takes the agony out of living for Binx and Kate?"[20] Everyone reading the novel wants this answer to the search. For Percy, the answer was the Catholic Faith. However, a novelist should not make such assertions explicitly. The indirect method would be to issue such claims from the mouths of the overlooked or outcasts in the fiction, to have an apostle character who was as lowly as were the biblical Peter and John. The Catholic proclamations do not come from priests but from Binx's teenage half-brother, Lonnie.

Lonnie is a good choice for an apostle because he is young, disabled, and dying. As a teen, his beliefs are easily dismissed as the product of inexperience. His disability hides his wisdom from the world who would reject it. And, finally, his suffering make his words impossible to contradict. If he were to claim that, after his death, a friendly alien race was going to abduct him to their planet where he would be restored to perfect health, no one would want to argue with him. Binx observes that Lonnie "has the gift of believing that he can offer his suffering in reparation for men's indifference to the pierced heart of Jesus Christ" (*MG* 137). Such a belief would be confusing coming from Binx, but it is fitting for Lonnie. Readers should notice that Binx calls his belief a "gift," not a burden or a delusion. Binx's word choice hints that he himself will come to accept such a strange belief. Through Lonnie, Percy offers a possible answer to Binx's metaphysical quest.

The epilogue shows a Binx who now lives "transparently in God," to use Kierkegaard's language.[21] Outwardly, he appears to have conformed to his mother's and aunt's plans for him: he becomes a doctor and marries Kate. Not to mention, he has joined the Catholic Church. Inwardly, however, Binx is not the lost man that he was at the beginning of the novel. In Percy's words, he has jumped over the ethical sphere into the religious sphere. Despite his transformation, Binx refuses to make any authoritative claims about his recently accepted faith. He calls on Kierkegaard to back up his reticence: "I have not the authority, as the great Danish philosopher declared, to speak of such matters in any way other than edifying. [It] is not open to me even to be edifying" (237). Instead of *telling* the answers to Binx's search, Percy *shows* Binx's transformation in the final scene. As Lonnie lies dying in the hospital, Binx converses outside with the confused siblings who question him about death. They ask, "When Our Lord raises us up on the last day, will Lonnie still be in a wheelchair or will he be like us?" (240). Binx affirms the resurrection of his brother: "He will be like you" (240). Here is the greatest evidence for Binx's conversion; he professes his belief in the transcendent world, and not just any alternative vision but the same one put forth by his brother Lonnie earlier in the novel. Lonnie lives in full assurance of the realities of Catholic doctrine. He "uses the idiom of the catechism in ordinary speech" and partakes of the Eucharist as "a sacrament of the living" (163–64).

Percy intended that the ending of *The Moviegoer* pay tribute to his literary model Fyodor Dostoevsky, also a Christian and a novelist. After the dialogue about the resurrection, the children cry, "Hurray!" (*MG* 240). At the conclusion of *The Brothers Karamazov*, after the young Illyusha has died, Alyosha Karamazov explains the resurrection to the children mourning him at the graveside, to which they respond, "Hurrah!" Percy insists that his ending is a "commentary, or gloss" on this ending, a conscious "salute to Dostoevsky" (*Conversations* 66). While the method here is indirect, Percy regards Binx's assertion of resurrection seriously: "Like Alyosha, he tells the truth. He wouldn't have said, 'Yeah' if he didn't mean it" (66). Binx may have begun the novel as an Underground Man searching to find his way in the world, but he ends the novel in imitation of another of Dostoevsky's characters, Alyosha, who was, in the hands of the Russian novelist, to become a great saint. Perhaps Binx too may have such a destiny.

2
The Last Gentleman

Nobody but a southerner could have written *The Last Gentleman* (1966). Walker Percy's second novel is *Don Quixote* in twentieth-century America, a contemporary *Candide,* Dostoevsky's *The Idiot* reincarnate, and yet, despite all of the connections with these great literary precursors, the book speaks with a strong southern accent. Although *The Last Gentleman* shares a handful of themes with *The Moviegoer*—the loss of self, the Cartesian divide which casts us all as angels and beasts, the theodicy incited by a suffering child—this second novel is more comic than the first, and of all Percy's novels (except perhaps *Lancelot*), the most southern. The title refers to the protagonist's roots pulling at him as he continually seeks ways of being a southern "gentleman." Through the bumblings of this comic hero, Percy explores the inadequacies of myths of southern identity in tandem with the homogenizing effects of contemporary culture.

Robert Coles, Pulitzer Prize–winning child psychiatrist and longtime Percy friend, calls *The Last Gentleman* Percy's "longest" and "most ambitious novel."[1] Critic John Desmond agrees with Coles, writing, "Apropos Percy's broader and more ambitious thematic concerns, the fictional strategies of *The Last Gentleman* are far more complex than those of *The Moviegoer*."[2] Like Binx Bolling from *The Moviegoer,* Williston Bibb Barrett in *The Last Gentleman* is trying to find his way in the world; but in contrast to that of his existential precursor, Barrett's quest is external.[3] The protagonist ventures across the country from Northeast to Southwest, starting in New York, with a long detour through the South, and ending in Santa Fe. He is a modern-day Ulysses (which is coincidentally the name of his camper), journeying like the Greek hero to Ithaca (in Barrett's case, Ithaca, Mississippi). Throughout this journey, Barrett stands apart from those he encounters as an outsider and an observer. His perspective on the world, via a third-person point of view, casts the most familiar things as strange. Although all Barrett wants is to be normal, to settle down with a wife and live a life, as he often surmises, his oddity keeps him from feeling at ease in society, even when others include him. Whereas Binx's search was profoundly negative—how to alleviate despair and malaise—Barrett's desire is directed towards a more positive goal: how to be happy.

The novel opens with this young man thinking in Central Park. In his hands is a "Tetzlar" telescope, which he depleted nearly the entirety of his bank account to purchase and, according to the first page of the novel, will change the rest of his life. This instrument is a metaphor for Barrett's current state. Like Binx, Barrett struggles with attending to what is right in front of him. He suffers from the "predicament of modern man" as Percy found it described in an essay by another southern writer, Allen Tate.[4] According to Tate, the modern man believes the solipsism that "we create the world in the act of perceiving it."[5] Instead of seeing reality as it is and concluding that truth is what correlates with reality, the modern person assumes that the world is as he perceives it to be. Tate asserts, "For some reason most [modern people] have a hard time fixing their mind directly under their noses, and before they see the object that is there they use a telescope upon the horizon to see where it came from."[6] Percy borrows Tate's metaphor of the telescope as a symbol for Barrett's trouble with viewing the world.

Barrett is referred to as the "young man" for the first sixteen pages of the novel, with no given name, and throughout most of the novel as "the engineer," a moniker that refers to his literal job as a Macy's humidification engineer, and symbolically as one who "engineers" his life; as he says, "I shall engineer the future of my life according to the scientific principles and the self-knowledge I have so arduously gained from five years of analysis" (LG 41). He does not claim his name (what is meant by this is not yet clear) until the last pages of the novel (67, 79, 409). At twenty-five years old, Barrett has been a florist in Memphis, a Princeton student, served two years in the army, read law in Ithaca, and now, with a large inheritance from his father, has numerous possibilities for life—so many, in fact, that he feels immobilized. Like "The Misfit" or

Mr. Shiftlet from Flannery O'Connor's short stories, the engineer has lived a nomadic existence, moving from job to job and interacting with people in only partial roles, never in real community.[7] The engineer's autonomy and rootlessness threaten his identity. Without people with whom he may regularly and authentically engage, he is not Will Barrett but merely "the engineer."

Because of his lack of self-knowledge, the engineer adapts to the people surrounding him, becoming one of them. When around Ohioans, he imitates their accent. When around southerners or New Yorkers, he adopts their regional mannerisms. His ability to situate himself within a group and his "radar" for reading what people mean versus what they say cause him to be perpetually dislocated, not at home even within his self. Add to this displacement a psychological disorder that Barrett calls his "nervous condition" that induces spells of amnesia, and you have a man to which "[e]verything looked strange. . . . Like the sole survivor of a bombed building, he had no second hand opinions and could see things afresh" (*LG* 11). Ironically, these spells are more of an unwanted gift than a curse. They grant him a renewed vision of the world. Additionally, his body signals to him when "there is something wrong" either with him or the world: his knee jerks, especially around beautiful women; he suffers bouts of *déjà vu*, and he occasionally lapses into fugue states (78). All of these symptoms indicate that all is not well.

Without family, a home, a job, or any ties to any community, Barrett cannot situate himself in the world. While he may pretend to play roles in the community with various groups, he cannot make heads or tails of life. As a child, he looked forward to becoming a man and knowing what to do and how to act, but now in his mid-twenties, he is disappointed. For "he still didn't know how to live" (11). His primary problem, as he diagnoses it, is another version of Percy's "hurricane theory": "he felt bad when other people felt good and good when they felt bad" (22). For instance, in the midst of an actual hurricane, Barrett observes how happy he is: "The hurricane blew away the sad, noxious particles which befoul the sorrowful old Eastern sky. . . . Everything was yellow and still and charged up with value" (25).[8] With the inclement weather wreaking havoc and increasing one's awareness of mortality, Barrett feels more alive. He observes this phenomenon several times over the course of his journey—how uncomfortable he feels in good environments and how good he feels in frightening or distressing situations. Observing that others feel this way without acknowledging it, Barrett diagnoses himself as peculiar. Thus, he wonders how he will ever live like a normal person. Will he ever be able to succeed at what he believes he wants—to fall in love, marry a wife, and live a life?

Barrett's definition of normal comes from the magazines he reads, the columns by "experts" on self-improvement, and the analyst he has been seeing for the past five years. Percy draws from his own experience seeing a psychoanalyst in New York when he was a medical student at Columbia, but he satirizes Barrett's relationship with this doctor, Dr. Gamow.[9] Dr. Gamow, who relishes Freudian slips and truthfully dislikes his patient, plays the part of the analyst as much as Barrett conducts the role of the amiable patient. According to Dr. Gamow, Barrett has a "defective ego structure" (38). Using clinical language, he describes Barrett's peculiar concern with "hollow men, noxious particles, and ultimate truths" (39). While those terms may sound ridiculous, the unseen realities observed by the strange engineer have more validity in a Percyean world than the psychoanalytic categories listed by Dr. Gamow. Although Barrett terminates his analysis under Dr. Gamow, he has no way to replace the analyst's method of engineering his life.

In addition to being called "the engineer," Barrett is referred to as "the Southerner" or the "Last Gentleman." Barrett is the "last of the line" of southern gentlemen whose prepackaged values have gradually been whittled away (3–5). By demythologizing the sources of white southerners' claims to aristocracy, W. J. Cash confronts the reigning tradition that exercises an unsubstantiated authority over the behavior of those residing in the South.[10] Although not a proponent of the Old South's mindset and an outspoken denouncer of the means of southern traditionalists, Percy highlights the ideals of the southern past that should not be shirked. In a 1957 letter to the editor of *America*, Percy writes:

There *is* a Southern heritage, and it has nothing to do with the colonel in the whiskey ad. It has to do with the conservative tradition of a predominantly agrarian society, a tradition which at its best enshrined the humane aspects of living for rich and poor, black and white. It gave first place to a stable family life, sensitivity and good manners between men, chivalry toward women, an honor code, and individual integrity. (*Signposts* 91)

Much of Percy's belief regarding the southern way was inherited from his guardian, Uncle Will, who was not only a planter but also a lawyer and a poet. This renaissance ancestor protected the agrarian way of life while also fighting for the rights of the impoverished and cultivating the good life with Brahms and Shakespeare, as Ed Barrett, Will's father, does in the novel. Will Percy considered nobility the end goal of all his actions, despite his faulty assumptions about racial and social hierarchy.[11]

It is the stalwart conviction in moral right and wrong that Percy looks back to through the nostalgic desires of Will Barrett. Where are steadfast gentlemen of chivalric character? Instead, the southern code of honor has been overcome by the "economic victory of the Sunbelt and the ongoing Los Angelization of the Southern community" (*Signposts* 166). With the commercialization of values and homogenization of culture, the South is dwindling into No-Place. Like its northern counterpart or even the blank potential of the Southwest, the South is relinquishing its distinctiveness to make way for golf courses, country clubs, and condominiums. The narrator notes, "The South [Barrett] came home to was different from the South he had left. It was happy, victorious, Christian, rich, patriotic, and Republican" (*LG* 185). Rather than licking their wounds over the Civil War, this culture has chosen to cash in on its mythical past for commercial gain.[12] Percy saw the "defeat and a tragic sense of history" as the South's "chief claim to uniqueness" (166). However, this South no longer exists. The South that "the last gentleman" confronts is not the Old South of *Gone with the Wind* nor the New South fantasized and idealized by 1930s Agrarians but a place that has disregarded the lessons of history.[13]

If readers compare another southern novel, such as Mark Twain's *Adventures of Huckleberry Finn*, with *The Last Gentleman*, they will see how much the southern landscape changed over a century, most notably in terms of racial conflict.[14] William Rodney Allen views Barrett's journey in *The Last Gentleman* as a revival of Huck's trip along the Mississippi River.[15] Allen relies on the travels of Huck Finn to provide the metaphor that connects the seemingly disparate scenes of Barrett's voyage. For instance, in Twain's bildungsroman, the young Huck befriends the runaway slave Jim, whereas Barrett catches a ride with a "pseudo-Negro" named Forney Aiken (*LG* 130), a New York journalist undercover as a black man and heading South to see the situation from an insider's perspective. Aiken parodies John Howard Griffin's 1961 *Black Like Me*, in which Griffin passes as a black man as he hitchhikes through the South in order to expose racial injustice from firsthand experience. The book was also made into a 1964 film released during the time of Percy's writing *The Last Gentleman*. By satirizing Griffin's account, Percy exposes the inadequacy of a white man claiming to understand black experience simply by temporarily changing his superficial exterior.

Although Percy was not primarily a "racial activist," he believed it was impossible for a southern writer not to address the "issue of race" in his fiction (*Conversations* 17). In a 1968 interview, following the publication of *The Last Gentleman*, Percy claimed, "I am completely convinced of the rightness of the Negro struggle for civil rights. My writing I think reflects this and I don't mind saying so" (*Conversations* 17). Most critics have focused on Percy's nonfiction, his essays decrying segregation, or his interviews where he explicitly denounces white southerners for being more Stoic than Christian. However, *The Last Gentleman*, especially in its attempts to address southern identity, reflects Percy's affirmation of the civil rights movement. Farrell O'Gorman writes, "Will must confront his heritage and struggle with the question of his responsibility for it. As in *The Moviegoer*, questions of racial justice here are finally bound up with the protagonist's moral—and finally religious—development."[16] Barrett has been separated from the racial tension in the South by his volitional exile in the North; yet, his return to the South forces him to consider not only his thoughts on the issue but also the necessity of his response.

Over the course of his southern homecoming, Barrett interacts with a number of African Americans as well as prejudiced white southerners, moments that are paid little critical attention but, as O'Gorman indicates, they showcase Barrett's moral development.[17] Upon his initial arrival in the South, Barrett sympathizes with David Ross, the Vaught family servant. Later, he is patronized by D'lo, his aunt's servant, who recalls Dilsey from Faulkner's *The Sound and the Fury*, and he observes with fascination the relationship between his Uncle Fannin and his servant Merriam, who plays the part of servant but actually relates to Barrett's uncle more like a brother would.[18] This list is not exhaustive. Allen believes the "climax of the racial theme in the novel"[19] occurs when Will and his love interest, Kitty Vaught, witness a riot on her college campus, an event that models the 1962 disturbance at the University of Mississippi when the first black student, James Meredith, was admitted. More significant than this fictionalized historical moment, however, is the scene when Barrett helps "pseudo-Negro" Aiken and his liberal crew to escape the law (*LG* 132). For the first time in the narrative, Barrett moves from observer of racial inequality to active opponent. Barrett has been accosted by Aiken and his friends, who are hiding in a bar, when Beans Ross, the stereotypical racist local cop, enters the picture. Although he intends to arrest Aiken and his troublesome instigators, Ross instead knocks out the black bar owner. In response, "Will takes his first dramatic action of the novel" and knocks out Ross.[20] Percy, who shares so much biographically with Will Barrett, perhaps acts out his own frustration with racial discrimination.

Although Barrett desires to embody notions of southern ethics and follow its code of honor, for the majority of the novel he does "not know what to think" (10). While his great-grandfather "knew what was what and said so and acted accordingly and did not care what anyone thought" (9), the next generations cannot be certain. Still-brave men such as Barrett's father wish more than anything else "to act with honor and to be thought well of by other men" (10). Integrity has given way to reputation. Barrett recalls walking with his father, who spoke romantically of "the galaxies and of the expanding universe and tak[ing] pleasure in the insignificance of man in the great lonely universe" (309). His father would recite "Dover Beach," Matthew Arnold's famous poem about the loss of faith, or tell stories about Barrett's grandfather and his great deed staring down the Grand Wizard of the Ku Klux Klan (310). The voice of his father reigns in his head, reminding him of an "Edenic past, a lost world of honorable men and faithful servants and virginal women," as Michael Kobre puts it.[21] Percy quotes Kierkegaard in the epigraph: "If a man cannot forget, he will never amount to much." Barrett seems unable to forget or let go of the idealized past, most specifically of his father. The loss of his father haunts Barrett as much as the loss of his did Binx in *The Moviegoer*. For the last gentleman, not having a father amounts to not having a model to follow in order to know how to live and be in the world.

Percy establishes Barrett as a case study of a wayfarer unaware of his own wayfaring status. Although Barrett begins in New York, he is no more at home among the Yankees and liberals, as he refers to them, than among the "splendid fellows" in his former homeland (*LG* 313). By the end of the novel, he finds himself in New Mexico, a place of "pure possibility [where] what a man can be the next minute bears no relation to what he is or what he was the minute before" (356). Percy claims, "Barrett's amnesia suggests a post-Christian shakiness about historical time" (*Conversations* 13). Because he cannot locate himself in place and time—often forgetting what year it is or unable to tell where he is—Barrett has become "a watcher and a listener and a wanderer" (*LG* 10). He does not profess any belief with certitude, and rather than act, he exists. He lives in limbo, always waiting for something to happen. "Waiting is the thing. Wait and watch," he tells himself (241). *Wait* becomes Barrett's motto.

Barrett's journey begins, and the action of the novel commences, when he is invited to return home to the South. His telescope indirectly introduces him to the Vaught family, beginning with the pretty Kitty Vaught, whom he sees through the lens and with whom he falls in love. Unlike Binx Bolling, Barrett is an orphan. His father committed suicide, an issue that will remain unresolved for Barrett until he is in his late forties, in the novel's sequel, *The Second Coming*. Although Barrett returns home midway through the novel, he does not speak to his aunts, even requesting that their cook keep silent about his visit, and his short time at his uncle's home is of no significance to his quest for happiness.

Instead, it is his adoptive family that becomes his primary interaction with community. The Vaught family are stereotypical 1960s Los Angelized southerners. They live in a castle on the golf links in a rich Alabama suburb. Mr. Vaught has commodified the South and uses its romantic myths to his advantage: at his Chevrolet agency, he dresses his salesmen in Confederate costumes. Mrs. Vaught is a conspiracy theorist whose southern penchant for local gossip has now been channeled towards "Bavarian Illuminati," the evils of fluoridation, and the real stories behind the South's defeats in the Civil War. And, unfortunately for Barrett, his lovely coed, Kitty Vaught, is not immune to the temptations of the new South—she is a sorority girl devoted to Alabama football who cares little for the outdated "lady-whore" dichotomy. Her driving motivation is to marry Barrett and settle down in a house overlooking the subdivision.

Barrett's attraction to Kitty may confuse the reader who expects the story to unfold according to the formula of a romantic comedy. However, we have to remember that the book is a satire, so this romance will unfold rather ironically. After all, Barrett falls in love with Kitty "at first sight and at a distance of two thousand feet" (*LG* 7). Loving at a distance is easy; it is the daily and up-close love that is difficult. Whenever mentioning Kitty, Barrett uses clichéd phrases from romance films, such as "his better half" or "his sweetheart" or, most frequently "charms in his arms." Although Barrett fantasizes about the sweetness of Kitty, when he is with her, everything about her rubs him the wrong way. He doesn't approve of her sexual forwardness, her desire to conform to everyone around her, and her affectation of a southern belle. In his eyes, she transforms from the "solitary girl on the park bench [who was] as inward and watchful as he" to "Miss Katherine Gibbs Vaught" who cannot wait to "have her picture in the *Commercial Appeal*" (259–60). Barrett disapproves of her supposed change when, in reality, only his view of her has changed. While before he saw her at a distance, now that he knows her closely, she does not fit his imagined perception.

The other Vaughts adhere even less to Barrett's preconceived images of them. Sutter and Val Vaught leave him perpetually perplexed, and Rita Vaught, Sutter's ex-wife, becomes an unwanted nemesis. Rita and Sutter both suffer from the Cartesian split, experiencing what Percy will later refer to as "angelism-bestialism" (*LIR* 382).

Rita is a feminist bisexual enamored with all things exotic and spiritual—other than Christianity. When Barrett visits her apartment one night to see Kitty, who is rooming with Rita, he finds them dressed in homespun Chamula hupil, drinking hikuli tea (aka peyote), draped in Navaho blankets, surrounded by grotesque votive paintings and discussing Huichol Indian rites. In his journal addressed to Val, Sutter calls Rita a "transcendent" person (*LG* 350). She "canonizes herself" as a "secular saint" who seems unselfish, but in reality she derives pleasure from being thought so. Under the guise of "love," Rita helps those in need because it makes her master over other people's destinies (350). As Sutter describes her, she lives a "self-actualizing" life, cultivating "joy, zest, awe, freshness, and the right balance of adult autonomous control and childlike playfulness" (246). Rita is a "spiritual" person in the 1960s hippie, mystical definition of the term. However, the "most urgent symptom" of Rita's "angelism" is "obsessive genital sexuality" (*Signposts* 223). She desires to seduce Kitty, and by the end of the novel, has lured Myra Thigpen to New York to live with her.

Diametrically opposed to Rita's spiritual nature is Sutter Vaught, who focuses on the physical nature of human beings. Sutter is a doctor, so the body is his medium. He knows all of its parts—the composition of blood, bone, gray matter, and so forth. As a scientist, he falls prey to the transcendent problems that Percy discussed via Binx in *The Moviegoer*. The scientist levitates above the concerns of the average person, dwelling in the realm of possibility. However, with only a belief in the existence of matter, the materialist scientist is limited to find methods of reentry via the physical world. Percy offers two alternatives to this kind of materialist scientist: violence or sex. Only these outlets will bring this scientist back down to earth and resituate him in the immanent world. Sutter embodies both *thanatos*, the death drive, and *eros*, the sex drive.

Rita castigates Sutter for his "deliberate cultivation of destructiveness, of [his] death-wish, not to mention [his] outhouse sexuality" (*LG* 242). When Barrett first meets him, he is firing a pistol merely for the exhilaration of it. Their first discussion is about fornicating. His journal fleshes out all the methods of sexual, genital reentry into the physical world, and he publishes articles on "The Incidence of Post-orgasmic Suicide in Male University Graduate Students," which uses Percyean language—via Kierkegaard—about transcendence, immanence, and reentry. Although he is the most explicitly sexual character of *The Last Gentleman*'s cast, his exploits were "left annoyingly vague" for the taste of 1960s readers, such as reviewer Walter Goodman.[22] "Sex is central to the book," Goodman notes, "but it is treated with such a courtly reticence." One has to remember that in the year *The Last Gentleman* was published, Jacqueline Susann's salacious *Valley of the Dolls*, with its soap-opera plot full of sex, drugs, abortions, and suicide, topped both *New York Times* and *Publisher's Weekly* bestseller lists, suggesting that Percy's contemporaries preferred less modest approaches to sexual forays.

Sutter records all of his philosophical observations in a notebook addressed to his sister Val. Percy used the "notebook" idea before: in *The Moviegoer*, Binx jots down his observations on his search. For Percy, Sutter's notebooks replace Dostoevskian dialogues, lengthy conversations about good and evil, sex and love, politics and religion, life and death. They present all of Sutter's grand ideas on how to live life, reflecting his Cartesian dualism. In interviews, Percy casts Sutter as "a queer sort of apostle" (*More Conversations* 143). Midway through the novel, Sutter bequeaths the journal to Barrett, and it becomes a kind of road map or existential bible for him. Although Barrett confers upon Sutter the authority of an apostle, and is ready to hear his message and live accordingly, Sutter never offers any transcendental news. His ruminations stay within the worldly sphere, and he rejects Barrett's requests for advice on how to live.

In contrast to Rita's and Sutter's dualistic personalities is Val Vaught, the eldest Vaught, who becomes the only example of un-bifurcated living in the novel. She has joined a religious order in South Alabama, working with black children who have gone mute in response to parental neglect. Val epitomizes the Christian response to the "race problem."[23] O'Gorman points out how she distinguishes between Barrett's father's Stoic stance for civil rights and her Catholic approach. Val tells Will, "Once I heard your father make a speech to the D.A.R. on the subject of *noblesse oblige* and our duty to the Negro" (*LG* 208). Val contrasts Ed Barrett's reasons for serving the Tyree children with her own. Whereas his actions countered the racism of his generation, his motives continued to perpetuate the problem. Ideologically, Ed Barrett presumed white superiority and adhered to a flawed Stoicism, similar to that of Aunt Emily from *The Moviegoer*. However, Val devotes her life to what Ed Barrett calls the "Negro cause" because she believes in racial equality and desires to upend racial injustice. Because, as Val will later confess, she received life from the Catholic Church, she desires to offer it outwardly to others—to the children, as well as to Barrett.[24]

While Barrett seamlessly stitches himself into most social situations, he cannot fake his way into conversation with Val. He thinks, "It was still impossible to get a fix on her" (*LG* 210). She demands authenticity, which is befuddling to Barrett. He grows angry when talking to her and blames it on her "perverse manner" rather than his own (297). When he visits her in Tyree County, he thinks: "I could see [the falcon in Central Park] better at one mile than this creature face to face" (301). Barrett is frustrated by his inability to reduce Val to a type or to emulate her way of being in the world as precisely as he does everyone else.

Unlike the divided selves of the other characters, Val has accepted a way of being whole and in the world. When she was a student at Columbia, someone asked her forthrightly, "[H]ow would you like to be alive" instead of "half dead"? (300). She assents and joins an order of nuns. "I believe the whole business," Val informs Barrett, "God, the Jews, Christ, the Church, grace and the forgiveness of sins" (301). Val sounds an awful lot like the author in her answer. When Percy is questioned, "Why are you Catholic?" he answers: "The reason I am Catholic is because I believe what the Catholic Church proposes is true" (*Signposts* 66). Val may act as Percy's mouthpiece in these scenes, offering a Catholic method for engineering one's life as an alternative to the new-age spiritualism of Rita, the sexual ethos of Sutter, or Barrett's southern manners. For the second half of the novel, her desire to see her youngest brother, Jamie, baptized drives the plot.

Jamie Vaught is sixteen, has been diagnosed with myelogenous leukemia, and has approximately four months to live. Like Barrett, he observes others in order to discover how to situate himself in the world, to figure out how to live, or, more accurately, how to die. His siblings each propose advice on the best plan to carry out his final days based on their separate ways of viewing the world. In one discussion on his behalf, Rita insists, "I desire for Jamie that he achieve as much self-fulfillment as he can in the little time he has. I desire for him beauty and joy, not death" (*LG* 244). To which Sutter sarcastically responds, "That is death" (244). Suffering from their divided natures, Rita and Sutter can only see part of Jamie. They view him either as a soul or a body, but they never see him holistically. Jamie becomes an object of the tug-of-war between their oppositional worldviews. Despite their attempts to vie for disparate methods of engineering Jamie's last moments, only Val's request for his baptism will succeed.

Near the final pages of the novel, Jamie Vaught is baptized. However, the moment is not triumphant, as you might expect from a Catholic author. Rather, the scene mixes the sacramental with the vulgar in unsavory ways. Following Val's admonition, Barrett calls a priest, Father Boomer, to Jamie's bedside to perform the ritual. In and out of consciousness, Jamie whispers, mumbles, and even rises from the bed momentarily to move his bowels. The foulness of the diarrhea overwhelms the scene, so that everything else happening—the priest's professions of the doctrines of the faith, Jamie's admission of faith, and the sacrament itself—seem profaned. Either this scene comically undermines Val's Catholicism or it suggests a third way, a *tertium quid* to Sutter's and Rita's nihilistic views of death. The interpretation of the moment hinges on Jamie's question to the priest, "Is that true?" (403). The priest has summarized the Catholic Church's beliefs about the purpose of human life, echoing what Val earlier proclaimed: "God exists and made you and loves you and that He made the world so that you might enjoy its beauty and that He himself is your final end and happiness, that He loved you so much that He sent His only Son to die for you and to found His Holy Catholic Church so that you may enter heaven and there see God face to face and be happy with Him forever" (403). If the priest's claims are true, then the baptism is redemptive; Jamie will be resurrected, and the ending here is hopeful. However, if they are not true, then the ending fails not only in its hope but also in its comedy.

Throughout the novel, the question repeatedly arises regarding who knows the truth about how to live and on what authority they speak. Kierkegaard's essay "Of the Difference between a Genius and an Apostle" convicted Percy to join the Catholic Church, and Percy, as a novelist, prescribes to the limits of a genius. In *The Last Gentleman* Percy uses Kierkegaard's explanation of an apostle's authority as the driving motivator for Val's, Father Boomer's, and ultimately, Jamie's faith. The difference between the message of the genius and that of the apostle, according to Kierkegaard, has nothing to do with content. Rather, Kierkegaard asserts that "an Apostle is what he is through having divine authority. *Divine authority is, qualitatively, the decisive factor.*"[25] The words of the apostle are "from elsewhere," from the "transcendental sphere," and therefore not limited to the empirical world.[26] Whether someone understands the message perfectly or whether it is well expressed does not matter. "An Apostle has no other proof," Kierkegaard claims, "than his own statement, and at the most his willingness to suffer anything for the sake of that statement."[27] Consider the difference between Albert Einstein and John the Baptist in the Gospel accounts. Einstein must prove that his claims are true with experiments and equations. He has no desire to die for his assertions, nor would he give credit for his theories to anyone but himself. In the case of John the Baptist, you have a man who ate locusts and honey in the desert, who declares that God has told him that a messiah is coming now, douses people in the Jordan River, and ultimately is beheaded for his heterodox ways and challenges to the reigning establishment.

To compose the dialogue between the dying Jamie and the reluctant priest Father Boomer, Percy draws directly from Kierkegaard's argument concerning the apostle's authority. After the priest has explained the doctrines of the faith, Jamie questions why he should believe such things and how the father knows it is true. The priest, with his impatient sighs and distant manner, declares matter-of-factly, "'It is true because God Himself revealed it as the truth. [. . .] If it were not true,' he said to Jamie, 'then I would not be here. That is why I am here, to tell you'" (*LG* 404). Father Boomer does not speak on his own authority, but he claims to speak on behalf of a divine authority. The man himself carries little persuasion either in his personality or his bedside manner. Barrett even suggests that the priest's "certain style of talking" sounds like a game-show host saying, "Now that is the sixty-four-dollar question," an allusion to the 1940s version of *Who Wants to Be a Millionaire?* In spite of the apathetic messenger and his simple method of proclamation, however, the revelation itself maintains authority.

Over the course of the novel Barrett has been seeking such authority and for someone to instruct him in how to live, as the priest does for Jamie. He diagnoses himself: "[M]y problem is how to live from one ordinary minute to the next on a Wednesday afternoon" (355). Yet, Sutter recasts Barrett's problem as one of authority. From Sutter's perspective, Barrett cannot tell the difference between the apostle's message and that of the genius. Sutter writes to Val in his notebook:

> Let us say you were right: that man is a wayfarer . . . who therefore stands in the way of hearing a piece of news which is of the utmost importance to him. . . . So you say: Here is the piece of news you have been waiting for, and you tell him. What does Barrett do? . . . he will receive the news from his high seat of transcendence as one more item of psychology to throw into his immanent meat-grinder, and wait to see if he feels better. (353–54)

When no news has authority, when religious revelations are a dime a dozen, and the Christian doctrine merely one item among many from which to select, then the receivers choose to validate such messages by weighing their content, especially as they pertain to their own experiences. Barrett would only hear the Catholic option as one of many and only consider such an option if it was aesthetically pleasing, intellectually fulfilling, and curative to his temporal-spatial disorder.

Percy acknowledges this problem as an author. He wants to be a "moralist and propagandist," as he tells Caroline Gordon, who will "tell people what they must do and what they must believe if they want to live."²⁸ However, Percy struggles with readers who are all Barretts, postmodern secularists who find no authority in the message that he preaches. As Anthony Burgess says of *The Last Gentleman* in his 1966 review, "Like all of Percy's books, this one is fundamentally unsatisfying. [His] books are all pathology and no cure."²⁹ The message that Percy intended to put forward to tell people how to live, that of Val and Father Boomer, is lost among the many alternatives that he presents through Rita, Sutter, and of course, Barrett.

The novel concludes ambiguously, both tragically and comically, and without any real sense of closure for Barrett. Jamie dies, but unlike Lonnie's death from *The Moviegoer*, there is no affirmation of resurrection or any evidence that his baptism offers hope. Sutter carries a pistol in his pocket, intending to kill himself, a plan that Barrett interrupts by professing his need for Sutter. However, whether this is the beginning of a beautiful friendship or merely a postponing of the inevitable remains unclear. The epigraph from Romano Guardini seems to signal the former: "Love will disappear from the face of the public world, but the more precious will be that love that flows from one lonely person to another." The scene has even been viewed as a reversal "of the night of [Barrett's] father's suicide, when lawyer Barrett rejected his son's plea to wait, rejected the boy's need and love in favor of suicide."³⁰ After all, Barrett calls himself by name for the first time, locates his self in himself, and in this moment, he acts rather than waits.

Yet, not enough information has been given that everything is going to be all right from here on out. One reviewer laments, "When the hero finally heads back toward his native Alabama to sell Chevrolets, it is not at all because he has discovered that he belongs there, but because he has seen the alternative is suicide."³¹ Earlier in the novel, Barrett internally chastises Sutter for dealing in such extremes: "Where he probably goes wrong, mused the engineer sleepily, is in the extremity of his alternatives: God and not-God, getting under women's dresses and blowing your brains out" (*LG* 354). While the extremes may be discomforting, Percy does not offer a compelling third option in *The Last Gentleman*. The reader is left with the disconcerting sounds of "Los Angeles laughter" (260) with its false happiness and the echo of Ed Barrett's shotgun.

3

Love in the Ruins

The end of the world has been lamented repeatedly throughout history: in Mesopotamian culture, in ancient Rome when the barbarians ransacked the capital, in the headlines of British news during World War I. Every age has suffered crises that have pushed some prophets and artists to don metaphorical sackcloth and cry out, "This is the end!" Even now, the twenty-first century is rife with apocalyptic terror: genocide on every continent, slavery and the trading of human lives as purchasable goods, environmental problems that lead scientists to predict widespread extinction of various species within decades, not to mention civil wars, floods, earthquakes, and global terrorism. The question is, what to do when the world crashes down around you? How to live and love in the ruins of civilization?

In 1960s America, when Walker Percy was writing his third novel, *Love in the Ruins* (1971), the culture of free love, which embraced sex, drugs, and rock and roll, ironically became a culture of division and violence in America. As Jim Morrison sang the word "higher" on *The Ed Sullivan Show,* race riots broke out in Detroit. The same year that Elvis married Priscilla in Vegas, San Franciscans in the thousands protested the U.S. involvement in Vietnam. While President Johnson negotiated a Cold War with the Soviet Union, assassins on American soil shot down Robert Kennedy and Martin Luther King Jr. Such fragmentation and hostility at the large scale affected Percy directly; in 1970 he received bomb threats from the Ku Klux Klan for his testimony in federal court against the display of the Confederate flag at the local Covington High School. It was this topsy-turvy, apocalyptic setting that inspired Percy to write *Love in the Ruins.*

Unlike Percy's previous two novels, which were more or less realistic, *Love in the Ruins* is a science-fiction satire. Percy felt compelled as a novelist to call attention to the horrors to which people around him seemed oblivious. "What the novelist notices is not how awful the happenings are," Percy says, "but how peculiar it is that people don't seem to notice how awful the happenings are" (*Signposts* 156). To grab the attention of his apathetic readers, Percy chose a genre that would allow him to depict extremes, where he could caricature the characters, set carnivalesque scenes, and plot an adventure story with universal consequences. In this novel, Percy emulates his Catholic contemporary Flannery O'Connor, who insisted that for the hard of hearing, you must shout, and that for the near-blind, you must draw large startling pictures. *Love in the Ruins* is an intentionally startling picture that yells at Percy's blind and deaf readers.

In 1967 Percy wrote Shelby Foote an outline of what would become the plot of *Love in the Ruins*:

> I have in mind a futuristic novel dealing with the decline and fall of the U.S., the country rent almost hopelessly between the rural knotheaded right and the godless alienated left, worse than the Civil War. Of that and the goodness of God, and the merriness of living quite anonymously in the suburbs, drinking well, cooking out, attending Mass at the usual silo-and-barn, the goodness of Brunswick bowling alleys (the good white maple and plastic balls), coming home of an evening, with twin rubies of the TV transmitter in the evening sky, having 4 drinks of good sourmash and assaulting one's wife in the armchair etc. What we Catholics call the Sacramental Life. (*Correspondence* 129)

While Percy wanted to address the large-scale social issues in American society, he intended to contrast the world's destruction with the quiet simple life of an ordinary citizen. He tells Foote that he has in mind the "Little Way" of St. Theresa of the Little Flower.[1] Although Percy will attempt to compose an epic like *Don Quixote* or *Moby-Dick*—as he says earlier in the same letter quoted above—he will do so by depicting the small-scale "Sacramental Life" of his hero, who ultimately will be content with loving his wife, doing his job, and "showing a bit of ordinary kindness to people" (*LIR* 399).

It should be noted that Percy limits the world's end to the American landscape for much of the novel, even more narrowly to the fictional Feliciana Parish in Louisiana. When the novel begins, "our beloved old U.S.A. is in a bad way": "Americans have turned against each other; race against race, right against left, believer against heathen, San Francisco against Los Angeles, Chicago against Cicero" (17). The divisions are not only racial, political, and religious, but also familial and geographic. The blacks have divided between being caricatures of "Uncle Tom" servants or "turned mean as yard dogs" and joined Bantu guerillas in the swamplands surrounding town. The two political parties have each adopted the nickname given to them as an insult by the opposite party: the Knothead Party versus the LEFTPAPASANE, an acronym for "Liberty, Equality, Fraternity, The Pill, Atheism, Pot, Anti-Pollution, Sex, Abortion Now, Euthanasia" (18). Both parties reside in the ironically named Paradise Estates, a suburb bordered on one side by "Fedville," a federal complex that includes a hospital, medical school, geriatrics center, and "Love Clinic," a lab for psychosexual experiments; and on the other side by Honey Island Swamp, the home of "castoffs and rebels" and "disaffected folk" such as the Bantu guerillas and dropouts from Tulane. The narrator, Tom More, alludes to Yeats's "The Second Coming" when he reflects on his contemporary situation: "The center did not hold" (18). In other words, in this novel, all is division—or subdivision—and anarchy.

Dr. Tom More is the protagonist and narrator of *Love in the Ruins*, the only Catholic hero of any of Percy's novels, albeit a "bad" Catholic, meaning he does not love God and no longer participates in the sacraments of confession and the Eucharist.[2] He is a middle-aged alcoholic psychiatrist who suffers from depression and megalomania. More is the case study for all of the problems facing contemporary America. He is not a hero in any usual sense of the word. Instead, he is a poor reflection of us all: a man in search of love and happiness who does not know what either of those words means; a scientist caught up in all of the pretenses and delusions of science; and a psychiatrist who is in as much need of a cure as any of his patients. More is a wayfarer without destination, a man who believes in the doctrines of the Catholic Church but does not follow them. Unlike his namesake, Sir Thomas More (1478–1535), the sixteenth-century English martyr, Percy's More is no saint.

Percy pays tribute to the great medieval Italian poet Dante Alighieri (1265–1321), through whose *Inferno* Percy was trudging at the time of his drafting of *Love in the Ruins*. Dante's poem begins, "Midway along the journey of our life, I came to myself in a dark wood."[3] More's narrative begins, "Now in these dread latter days of the old violent beloved U.S.A. and of the Christ-forgetting Christ-haunted death-dealing Western world I came to myself in a grove of young pines" (*LIR* 3). Echoing the passivity of Dante's pilgrim, More also refuses responsibility for ending up where he has found himself. These two narrators awaken metaphorically in their respective dark woods without recollecting how the paths they chose led to their consequent destinations. In Percy's narrative, like Dante's, the world takes on an infernal quality, and the devil himself will appear as a Jewish salesman.[4] Moreover, as Dante in *The Divine Comedy* travels to paradise from earth via purgatory, and hell, so Tom "travels continually among the four settings," which Linda Whitney Hobson describes as "heaven [paradise], earth (town), purgatory (swamp), and hell (the pit)."[5] However, in Percy's "postmodern allegory," the pilgrim waivers between the realms, rather than resolutely climb heavenward. The journeying More may also recall John Bunyan's Christian from *Pilgrim's Progress*, but unlike these literary ancestors, More does not know that he is on a pilgrimage.

To More, he already resides in paradise, though an earthly one. This location betrays one of the major themes in the novel—the tension between the City of Destruction and the Celestial City, to borrow Bunyan's vocabulary, or the City of Man and the City of God, as St. Augustine would put it. The idea of the secular versus Christian city was very much on American readers' minds in the late 1960s. In 1965 Harvey Cox published *The Secular City*, a book that caused quite a stir and quickly attained multiple printings within its first year. Percy read and underlined his copy. Cox claims that the City of God may be accomplished through the City of Man. Through politics and good statesmanship, Cox contends, Christians may achieve a de-spiritualized version of God's kingdom, a "victorious new regime."[6] About 450 years before

Cox's book, Sir Thomas More published his book about paradise on earth entitled *Utopia*. The title plays with the two Greek spellings of the word, one of which means "good place" (*eu-topos*) and the other which means "no place" (*ou-topos*). Like More's Utopia, Cox's secular city may be a good place, but it is more likely a no place. These predecessor cities cast shadows on Percy's protagonist's "oasis of concord" and undermine the utopian descriptions of Paradise Estates where "everyone gets along" and houses "sparkle like jewelry" (*LIR* 16).

Like Binx and Barrett before him, More sees what others cannot, the signs that all is not well. For instance, More sees vines sprouting everywhere, but no one seems to notice. He alerts his neighbor "to the vines cracking his slab," but the man "seemed not to hear" and instead shows off his new lawn mower (10). In his speech "Novel Writing in an Apocalyptic Time," Percy says the novelist's job is to look for "fault lines in the terrain," for signs "that things have gotten very queer without anyone seeming to notice it, that sane people seem to him a little crazy and crazy people sometimes look knowledgeable" (*Signposts* 155). More is able to see the signs, but his singular vision marks him as potentially crazy. Like *The Moviegoer*, the novel is written in first person, but unlike Binx Bolling, this narrator is less than trustworthy. When More introduces himself to the reader, he is perched on a hill with his back against a tumored pine, waiting for the apocalypse and craning his neck for an alleged sniper. In an echo of Edgar Allan Poe's murderous narrator from "Tell-Tale Heart," More begins his story by offering a choice to the reader, "Either I am right and a catastrophe will occur, or it won't and I'm crazy" (*LIR* 3). More keeps the reader in suspense throughout the story: Is our narrator sane or crazy? Will the world end, or does Tom More need medical attention?

The action of the novel occurs between the first and Fourth of July, so the fated end of the world lines up nicely with the anniversary of the United States' independence. The narrative walks us backwards from the current predicament through the events that led to this point and then forward to a potential end of the world. Correlating with the fragmentation of the culture and the bifurcation and disorientation of the protagonist himself, the events are out of sync and jump between places and times. Whereas *The Moviegoer* and *The Last Gentleman* allowed time for the ruminations and gradual growth of the characters, *Love in the Ruins* begins the emphasis on the present. The first word of the novel is "now": "Now in these dread latter days. . . ." (*LIR* 3). The end of the world intensifies every moment in the novel and indeed adds pressure to readers to attend to their own "now" moment. While the novel was published in 1971 and set in 1983, its futuristic events seem prescient of the twenty-first century and will be relevant into the next millennium. For Percy recognizes that the end of the world may always seem to be happening *now*.

This particular end of the world has come about because of the prevalence of the fallacy of Descartes, the widespread adherence to Gnosticism, and Tom More's messianic pride. Percy has dealt with the Cartesian problem in both of his previous novels: Binx and Sutter both suffered from abstraction, locating themselves as transcendent above the world and casting everything as objects below them. More directly blames Descartes for the rent soul of "Western Man," saying that he "ripped the body loose from mind and turned the very soul into a ghost that haunts its own house" (*LIR* 191). As a psychiatrist, More has observed the division in his patients as well as in himself. More refers to it as "More's syndrome," which not only credits himself for the discovery of the condition but also suggest that he shares this sickness with his patients. He also calls it "angelism-bestialism" (382). More provides a series of case studies to prove how the problem is widespread. One patient, for instance, "has so abstracted himself from himself and from the world around him, seeing things as theories and himself as a shadow, that he cannot, so to speak, reenter the lovely ordinary world" (34). The condition is not relegated to a specific political, religious, racial, or generational group. Despite the divisions between Knotheads and Lefts, between blacks and whites, between fathers and sons, More detects angelism-bestialism as a universal dilemma.

We are either spirits or beasts, neither of which leaves any room for the Catholic belief that proposes humans are embodied souls. The scientists in *Love in the Ruins* are primarily behaviorists, descendants of B. F. Skinner (hence the "Skinner Box"), who believe that human beings are mere organisms that respond to environmental stimuli. Bad behaviors are thwarted by painful shocks, and good behaviors are promoted by producing pleasurable sensations in the patient. More throws the doctors a curve ball because he believes that some pleasures are bad, such as sex outside of marriage. For instance, when Max Gottlieb, one of the doctors at the hospital, attempts to fix More's problem, he offers to put More in the Skinner Box: "We could condition away the contradiction. You'd never feel guilt" (118). More responds unexpectedly, "Then I'd really be up the creek" (118). His guilty feelings over what he classifies as "sin" remind him of his unseen soul. More explains, "Unfortunately, there still persists in the medical profession the quaint superstition that only that which is visible is real. Thus the soul is not real" (29). Unlike his fellow scientists, More believes there is more to the human person than mind and flesh.

The two alternative perspectives of More and the other scientists come to blows literally in the scene in the middle of the book where Dr. More debates Dr. Buddy Brown over the patient Mr. Ives. The elderly man is mute and appears an invalid in need of a wheelchair. Before this condition, his behavior at the "Golden Years Senior Citizen Settlement in Tampa" was unseemly: he defecated on Flirtation Walk, cursed Ohioans, and was found digging for the Fountain of Youth on the putt-putt green. While Dr. Brown advises that the patient be dispatched to a euthanasia facility in Georgia, Dr. More argues there is nothing wrong with Mr. Ives, so the man should do as he pleases. More is able to show that Mr. Ives has been refusing to talk because he disagrees with the behaviorists' attempts to manipulate him. According to the scientists' dualistic thinking, people either respond mentally to reason or to pleasure and pain encountered by their flesh. They do not account for a free will that could allow people to act against their best interest. Mr. Ives is an anomaly in their system. Like Dostoevsky's Underground Man, Mr. Ives acts inappropriately to demonstrate his freedom.

Throughout *Love in the Ruins*, the scientists attempt to quell emotional responses that seem, in their behaviorist system, to be unwarranted—for instance, when Max tries to talk More out of feeling guilty for "fornication." The battle lines are drawn mostly in regard to sex and death, *eros* and *thanatos*, what Sigmund Freud called the two drives of human beings.[7] The Love Clinic and the Geriatrics Clinic (which practices euthanasia regularly) become war zones for More's controversy with the tenor of his time. At the Love Clinic, behaviorist scientists study sexual relations between subjects through a glass observation window and with "vaginal computers" and other devices. Sex is treated distantly, not as something emotional or moral (or, as Percy would think of it, sacramental), but as a "natural activity, like eating and drinking" (*LIR* 116). In introducing the Love Clinic, Percy contrasts a subject pleasuring herself and More's almost juvenile flirtation with one of the nurses, Moira. If the reader is uncomfortable with Percy's blatant descriptions of masturbation, he might have responded, "There is hope for the world yet." For Percy, the characters' lack of discomfort is worrisome because they have suppressed their natural emotional and moral responses to what sex ought to be and have bought into the belief that sex is only a physical act.

Percy considered titling the novel "How to Make Love in the Ruins," which highlights its sexual theme and the misunderstanding of the word "love" by the majority of the characters. For those who work at the Love Clinic and the "love community" that lives in the swamp, "love" is demoted to refer only to sex. More himself wavers with his use of the word. Whereas More once "loved" his wife, Doris, meaning her whole person—body, mind and soul—he now "loves" any beautiful, young female, meaning only that he desires them sexually or romantically. When More analyzes his attraction to Doris, he wonders, "Was it her slight maleness, long-leggedness . . . that set my heart pounding over breakfast? No, that's foolishness. I loved her, that's all" (*LIR* 65). Through most of the novel, More locates his love in his tingling scalp or sacrum and cannot distinguish between his love of Moira Schaffner; Lola Rhoades; or Ellen Ogelthorpe, his secretary and nurse who becomes his second wife. At the end of the novel, More's "heart leaps with love" for Ellen (384). The site of love insinuates a change in the meaning of the word for More.

Just as the generation in the novel has lost the meaning of *eros*, so too has it lost the ability to deal with death, with *thanatos*. While discussions of sex are blatant, words like "funeral" bring about blushing, and girls "try to pull their dresses down over their knees" (224). "Death" is impolite in civil conversation in these "latter days," despite the rampant murdering by Bantus and manifold executions by "qualitarians (= euthanasiasists)" (219). As in *The Moviegoer* when Binx observes that words "are worn out" (162), More lives in a culture in which the "meanings" of words "have slipped" (*Signposts* 248). Percy will return to this theme with greater fervor in both *The Second Coming* and *The Thanatos Syndrome*. Because death, and its often prerequisite, suffering, embarrasses people, they choose pseudonyms and discuss abstract principles such as "'freedom,' the 'dignity of the individual,' the 'quality of life,' and so on" (*Signposts* 248) to talk around the reality of death in all its forms.

Only More discusses death without awkwardness and refuses to circumvent the issue. In this way, Tom More is a credit to his namesake, who Percy asserts was "most cheerful with Brother Death in the neighborhood" (*MIB* 109). More has been near to death. Before the events of the novel, he attempted suicide, and it made him "love life" (*LIR* 97). After the death of his daughter, Samantha, and the subsequent loss of his wife, Doris—who left him for an Englishman, fled to Mexico, and died there—More slashes his wrists. Yet, the minute he sees the blood, More revives: "I came to myself, saw myself as itself and the world as what it is and began to love life" (97). He checks himself into the mental ward at the hospital, where he technically remains a patient throughout the novel, though not confined to the building. His status as an "ex-suicide" should grant him greater perspective; however, like Kate Cutrer in *The Moviegoer*, More wavers between terror and gratitude for life.

More responds to his terror, brought on by Cartesian displacement, by chasing women and numbing his pain with Early Times whiskey. "Man is not made for suffering," More tries to convince himself (*LIR* 337). Yet, when Dr. Buddy Brown protests that euthanasia prevents suffering, More claims that he prefers suffering. In fact, More did permit his daughter to suffer, despite his wife's protests to take her to Lourdes for a cure. When More recalls Samantha's death, he asks for her forgiveness: "Samantha, forgive me. I am sorry you suffered and died, my heart broke" (374). Then, More inserts this strange addendum, "but there have been times when I was not above enjoying it" (374). In these lines, More joins Binx and Barrett, who proposed that people feel most alive in the midst of suffering. "Is it possible," More wonders, "to live without feasting on death?" (374). This, again, is Percy's hurricane theory. In this context, More's honest admission that he occasionally enjoyed his daughter's suffering seems preferable to those blushing students who pretend that death does not exist. Percy is showing the problem with those who pursue physical pleasure as the consummation of happiness: for those individuals, suffering and death are inadmissible realities.

After Samantha's death, More's family life falls apart. Doris and he choose incompatible ways to deal with the death. They buy into the lie that they are either angels or beasts: as Doris becomes more angelic, Tom determines to become more bestial, until their marriage dissipates. More blames Doris's mysticism on the books that she turns to: *Siddhartha*, *Atlas Shrugged*, and *ESP and the New Spirituality*. "God, if you recall, did not warn his people against dirty books," More says. "He warned them against high places" (*LIR* 63). In his depiction of Doris, the "priestess of high places" who sets off with her spiritual mentor, Alistair Fuchs-Forbes, to go find herself in Cozumel, Percy foresees the burgeoning self-help and self-love culture. Critic Brian Smith sees Doris's enlightenment as "exemplified today in popular books like Elizabeth Gilbert's *Eat, Pray, Love* [which] authorizes a flight from all the restraints of our ordinary life" (*Political Companion* 187). Doris rejects her husband because he reminds her of the loss of their daughter, and she refuses to make love because, as a physical act, it is lowly and detracts from her newfound spirituality. Although Doris wants to find herself as well as true love, her choices excise her from community and thus remove her opportunity for real love.

Doris's and Tom's different responses to death illustrate the Cartesian fallacy, which More sees as a precursor to the approaching apocalypse. A second herald of the apocalypse is Gnosticism, a second-century heresy that locates evil outside of the human person, where it can be solved with one's own resources. In his essay "Walker Percy and Modern Gnosticism," Cleanth Brooks emphasizes two crucial aspects of the heresy that he pulls from Eric Voegelin: "(1) Man the creature is not responsible for the evil in which he finds himself. He has a right to blame it on someone or something else [. . .]. And (2) Man's salvation depends on his own efforts."[8] It is the belief that humans are not to be blamed for their actions, especially their weaknesses and failings, combined with the unalterable trust that there are ways of fixing all of our problems and improving ourselves—the right drug, the right weight-loss program, the right religion, and so on. Most Americans in the twentieth and twenty-first centuries are Gnostics. In *Bad Religion*, the *New York Times* editorialist Ross Douthat claims that the Gnostic heresy "has a mass following that far exceeds the Sunday attendance at every Mainline denomination."[9] Harold Bloom has called Gnosticism "The American Religion."[10]

In *Love in the Ruins*, Percy predicts the rise of Gnosticism, for most characters are incognizant Gnostics, including Tom More himself. More classifies his mother as a "Catholic Gnostic": "Though she believes in God, she also relies on her crystal ball" (*LIR* 177). She solves her problems with astrology, interprets scripture in whatever way justifies her own beliefs, and has left the Roman Catholic Church for the American Catholic Church, for which "Property Rights Sunday is a major feast day," and the banner outside the building depicts Christ "holding the American home, which has a picket fence" (181).[11] Although More seems to snarl at his mother's Gnosticism, he showcases his own unconscious adoption of the heresy in his devotion to science and his messianic pride.

Not only does More believe that paradise can be created by science here on earth, but he also assumes that he will be this creator. More has invented a Qualitative-Quantitative Ontological Lapsometer, which can diagnose and treat problems in people's souls. "My little machine is the first caliper of the soul," More brags (106). He claims, "Now I know how to be happy and make others happy" (20). His machine works by tricking a person into believing that she or he feels happy. However, this only solves the problem of longing in an ephemeral way. In other words, it is a temporary high. The lapsometer fails to overcome the problem in people's souls. Unlike Percy's other heroes, More does not stand entirely outside the problem. Rather, he falls prey to the temptations of scientism, the belief that he can cure all evils with the resources of science. As a scientist himself, Percy did not disdain science. However, Percy embraces the word "scientism" to explain the common assumption that "in the face of the mysteries of life which confront [the layman], the mysteries of nature, his own health, indeed of his very self and his existence and the secret of his being—nothing seems more natural to him than that *they* know the answers. *They*, of course, are the scientists" (*Signposts* 297–98). In other words, in the modern consciousness, science is exalted to a throne that it cannot fill. If there is something wrong—whether physical, emotional, or spiritual aches and pains, people assume that science will have the answer. Although More suffers from the same disorder as his patients, in his arrogance he establishes himself as an expert scientist able to treat others.

The problem, of course, is that More cannot "save the world" (*LIR* 382) because he is not God. His Gnosticism has robbed him of knowledge of his sinfulness, and thus made him easy prey for the demonic. Although More appears unable to deal with his sin, he recognizes that "most people nowadays are possessed, harboring as they do all manner of demonic hatred and terrors and lusts and envies, that principalities and powers are nearly everywhere victorious" (31). A fellow madman, Father Rinaldo Smith, agrees with More that devils are the cause. "They've won and we've lost," Smith laments (185). When his psychiatrist questions him further, the priest explains that the devils have won because people are now living-dead. Like Binx's repetitive cry that "men are dead, dead, dead" (*MG* 228), Smith observes, "I am surrounded by the corpses of souls" (*LIR* 186). Only this time, instead of the malaise, the devil is to blame. The demonic casts a strong presence over the entire narrative of *Love in the Ruins*, which seems appropriate for an apocalyptic novel and the "truly demonic age" in which Percy considers himself writing (*Signposts* 158).

In *The Death of Satan,* Andrew Delbanco informs us that the Gnostics believed Satan "was not a deceiver at all, but a giver of knowledge, the source of man's understanding," a trope that Percy plays with in *Love in the Ruins*.[12] Percy's satanic figure, Art Immelmann, is a comedic caricature. This demon has been appropriately linked to Mephistopheles in Faust, but he shares more in common with Dostoevsky's devil from *The Brothers Karamazov*. As though summoned, Art arrives in the midst of a lightning storm while More sits at his office desk wishing that his "lapsometer could treat as well as diagnose" (*LIR* 165). He appears like a salesman with an old attaché case, an "odd-looking fellow, curiously old-fashioned" (166). Art comically masks his smell of brimstone with Ban deodorant and tries to play it modern with American attire, though his style is a couple of decades behind. His first appearance makes More bristle with frustration, but by the third meeting More has acquiesced to the strange man and signed a contract with him.

More has made a pact with this devil, and thus brought about the potential apocalypse that we see him fearing at the start of the narrative. His habits of sin have exposed him to the demonic. Just as Doris opened the door to her subsequent fall by reading books on various forms of spirituality, so More has invited the devil into his life by trusting science too much, idolizing women and music, and ultimately exalting himself to the highest place. In the longest dialogue between Immelmann and More, Immelmann sounds as though he is speaking More's own thoughts: "Science to help all men and a happy joyous love to help women.... This love has its counterpart in scientific knowledge: it is neutral morally, abstractive, godlike—" (213–14). Immelmann unveils the satanic end of More's scientism: it attempts to play "god" to provide universal happiness. Yet, More is too far gone in his own system to denounce Immelmann. Instead, More allows the devilish Art to use the lapsometer on him, turning his invention against him. When Immelmann gifts lapsometers to careless users as a "pilot" program to test the device's success, More blames Immelmann for the wickedness that then transpires. But the fault is his.

With More's consent, Immelmann distributes the lapsometer to audience members attending the debate regarding Mr. Ives. Gary Ciuba describes the scene as though it occurs in Dante's *Inferno*:

> The amphitheater of the Pit becomes an infernal circle whose center does not hold. As the doctors, students, and nurses aim their new toys at each other, they release evil spirits of vague rage

and abstracted lust until they writhe like a den of vipers. Over the jumble of raised fists and spread legs presides Art Immelmann . . . who waves his arms like an old-time band leader.[13]

Instead of the madness leading to worldly destruction, however, things merely settle down. Max gives a shot to More to calm him down, and Ellen, his good nurse, returns him to his home for a good night's sleep. The infernal chaos fades as though it were a commercial break.

In fact, evil is continuously overlooked or ignored, despite the numerous dead bodies and burning homes. More escapes the Bantu attack on Paradise Estates by holing up with his three love interests at the ruins of a Howard Johnson's motel, where he has stowed away a collection of Great Books and nonperishable foods. Rather than confront the violence, More prefers to engage in meaningless trysts with his young women. His inability to confront the reality of the destruction recalls Percy's observation about society: "The numbers of innocent dead are huge but do not amaze. . . . One listens, looks, then tunes into a talk show where people get properly angry about potholes, labor unions, handguns, inflation" (*Signposts* 157). In a century of constant death tolls and a flood of media images of corpses, what else can one do but make love in the ruins? Yet, More's trysts leave him unsatisfied, and he cannot deny the sense that something is wrong.

Through More's unappeasable desires, Percy stresses the faultiness in any earthly definition of "pursuit of happiness." He has reincarnated St. Augustine in a twentieth-century American context. "The first thing a man remembers is longing," More insists, "and the last thing he is conscious of before death is exactly the same longing" (*LIR* 20). This admission places him squarely in the tradition of St. Augustine, who begins his *Confessions*, "Our hearts are restless, O God, until they rest in you."[14] The fourth-century Bishop of Hippo admits in his spiritual autobiography to chasing women, fame, and other trivial pleasures before finding his rest in God. Similarly, More has sought to fulfill his longing with women, scientific discovery, and alcohol, but nothing has quenched it. "I believe in God," More confesses, "but I love women best, music and science next, whisky next, God fourth, and my fellowman hardly at all"

(*LIR* 6). Augustine would diagnose More as suffering from disordered loves and a disintegrated self, if only the "bad Catholic" would listen. Percy himself attests, "the novel is only incidentally about politics. It is really about the pursuit of happiness" (*Signposts* 248). Through a case study of More's disordered desires, Percy diagnoses societal sickness. Much of what appears wrong in the world, in *Love in the Ruins*, can be pointed back to individuals' pursuits of false sources of happiness.

Before Samantha's death, More glimpsed the possibilities for human happiness whether or not vines are sprouting through the ruins. More remembers attending Mass with his daughter, partaking of the Eucharist, and then loving his wife. He claims, "[I]t took religion to save me from the spirit world, from orbiting the earth like Lucifer and the angels, that it took nothing less than . . . eating Christ himself to make me mortal again and let me inhabit my own flesh" (*LIR* 254). More emphasizes the Eucharist's role in reminding him that he was an embodied creature rather than an ethereal being like Lucifer and the angels. Also, the Eucharist, in which Christ's presence is manifest mysteriously under the appearance of bread and wine, integrates a person into the communion of saints that is also Christ's body. When More says that he was then able to return home after Mass and make love with his wife, he indicates his renewed sense of community and understanding of love as more than sex. Finally, the Eucharist demands confession as a necessary precursor. The act of confession would counter More's Gnosticism and messianism, for he would acknowledge his sinfulness. Without these sacraments, More has lost his mooring.

Although the novel feigns an approaching universal apocalypse, the actual battle has been over the soul of Tom More. More had associated himself with the devil earlier in the story when he suggested that he suffered from a tendency to orbit "the earth like Lucifer and the angels" (254). When Art releases the lapsometers to the attendees in the Pit, More renames "More's syndrome" as "Lucifer syndrome" (236). While More attempts to save the world from this demonic condition with his lapsometer, he admits that the only thing that saved him was the Eucharist. To win against the devil, then, More has to forego his scientism, his Gnosticism, and ultimately, his pride. He must stop trusting in his own ability to save the world and begin valuing others above himself. Appropriately, the devil is beat by More praying, "Sir Thomas More, kinsman, saint, best and dearest merriest of Englishmen, pray for us and drive this son of a bitch hence" (376). Grace intercedes, and Art Immelmann turns "slowly away, wheeling in slow motion" like the way a phantom would fade in an episode of *The Twilight Zone* (376). All returns to normal as though nothing has happened. As Ellen observes, "There was no real trouble. . . . Most people here . . . like things the way they are" (366).

The last section of the novel occurs five years after the interrupted "end of the world." Among the final images is More in a sackcloth over his sports coat with ashes in his hair, a member of the "remnant of the remnant" of the Roman Catholic Church, which More has compared to "stragglers after a battle" (187). More has returned to the church and is confessing for the first time in eleven years. Throughout the narrative, the problem for More has been a lack of guilt. More lives in a culture that denies sin, and thus disavows that human beings are to blame for their wrong actions. However, as a Catholic, More believes that, without guilt, he cannot confess, repent, or receive the Eucharist. Although More still does "not feel sorry" for his sins, he believes that, if he asks for forgiveness, his sins will be absolved (397). His lack of guilt perpetuates his pride and prevents his contrition.

If More is going to receive the sacraments and thus experience release from the devils that haunt him—both within and from without—he must acknowledge his sinful state. In the confessional with Father Smith, More begins to feel guilty for the first time. Father Smith attempts a few priest "tricks," as More calls them, and then scalds More with his direct reproach:

> Meanwhile, forgive me but there are other things we must think about: like doing our jobs, you being a better doctor, I being a better priest, showing a bit of ordinary kindness to people, particularly our own families—unkindness to those close to us is such a pitiful thing—doing what we can for our poor unhappy coun-

try—things, which, please forgive me, sometimes seem more important than dwelling on a few middle-aged daydreams. (399)

More confesses, "You're right. I'm sorry" (399). He admits to feeling "ashamed" for his sins (399). Notice that it was not a reminder of More's sins that compelled him to repentance. Rather, the priest first asks forgiveness from More, which More reciprocates. The humility of the priest provides a model for how More should respond. Moreover, the priest humbles More by calling him on his self-importance and determining that other "things" are more significant. More recognizes the truth of the priest's words and releases his grip on the high place on which he had set himself.

The world is still run by barbarians, but More now attempts a "Little Way" in the midst of it, "hoeing collards in [his] kitchen garden," an allusion to the final line of Voltaire's *Candide*, in which the protagonist advises us to tend to our own gardens (*LIR* 381).[15] The garden imagery has been prevalent throughout the story, as More fought with his misplaced attempts to recast a new Garden of Eden. In his book *Gardens*, Robert Pogue Harrison argues that human beings are meant to be gardeners, for "human happiness is a cultivated rather than a consumer good, that it is a question of fulfillment more than of gratification."[16] By tending to his garden, More shows that he has learned this lesson. He is now cultivating his happiness in the midst of ruins.

Whereas destruction and death once loomed over July Fourth, Christmas Eve heralds both the birth of Christ and the new life of Tom More. The timing of More's return to life is significant for two reasons. On Christmas Eve six years previously, More attempted suicide. However, now he has chosen life. Moreover, Christmas Eve in the Christian calendar is the night on which the Church looks forward to Christ's birth, the life that, in Christian teaching, will ultimately defeat death. By ending the novel on Christmas, Percy suggests that the reader can take comfort that More—at least for now—has defeated his demons.

Although Percy always asserted in interviews that it was not a novelist's job to be edifying, his goals in *Love in the Ruins* are, at least implicitly, to preach a better way of living to his readers. *Love in the Ruins* is perhaps the most didactic of all of Percy's novels, while still employing Kierkegaard's technique of indirection—satire, in this instance. But Percy writes a surrealist satire not to mock his current age. Rather, Percy intends to present the problems as he sees them in order to avoid perpetuating them. In an essay on writing apocalyptic fiction, Percy describes his agenda as "prophesy in reverse": "Perhaps it is only through the conjuring up of catastrophe, the destruction of all Exxon signs, and the sprouting of vines in the church pews, that the novelist can make vicarious use of catastrophe in order that he and his reader may come to themselves" (*Signposts* 118). Percy is like the ghost of Christmas future who granted nasty old Scrooge a vision of his dark fate, so that the frugal miser would awake a more generous man in the morning. The goal of this novel is that readers wake up, that we come to ourselves and realize we, like Dante or More, are in a dark wood and have lost the straight way. Percy hopes, like Dante or More, we can begin our ascent towards the eternally promised paradise that Catholics, good and bad, believe in.

4
Lancelot

The epigraph to *Lancelot* (1977) hints at how to read this strange, dark novel. Percy had been making his way through Dante's *The Divine Comedy*, a fourteenth-century Italian epic of a pilgrim's journey through hell to heaven, which influenced strongly Percy's third and fourth novels. When *Lancelot* was forming in Percy's mind, he began with Dante's opening lines, "I came to myself in the middle of my life" (*Correspondence* 175). Percy arranges his novel into nine chapters, paralleling the structure of Dante's hell, which is organized in nine circles. One of the earlier titles of the novel was "Lancelot in Hell." Like Dante the pilgrim, Percy intends to move his reader to the bottom of hell, which the protagonist, Lancelot Andrewes Lamar, terms, in an echo of Joseph Conrad, "the heart of darkness" (*L* 216).

Percy pulls his epigraph from *Purgatorio*, the second volume in Dante's trilogy, in which Dante's muse, Beatrice, explains to the reader why Dante's life necessitated this sojourn in the afterlife to save his soul. The extreme measures were taken because, as she says, "[Dante] sank so low that all means / for his salvation were gone, / except showing him the lost people. / For this reason I visited the region of the dead. . . ."[1] Percy intends to apply this situation to his reader. He is clarifying why he endeavored to explore the "region of the dead," the hellish interior world of Lancelot as well as the company he keeps before his ultimate fall. Told from the first person, *Lancelot* feigns a monologue—much like Dostoevsky's *Notes from the Underground*—that is actually a dialogue with a silent participant—much like Camus's *The Fall*. Percy intended to "allow the side of darkness to talk itself out in one long-winded rant."[2] The narrative itself is a form of confession, though a sacrilegious one without contrition from the penitent. It may also resemble a psychotherapy session, in which the interlocutor provides a sounding board for the patient. Lancelot's confessor or therapist is Percival, a former Catholic priest and childhood friend, who is called alternately Father John. This method of narration places the reader in the position of Percival. To offer potential salvation for Percival and for the reader who is situated as an invisible addressee of Lancelot's harangue, Percy exhibits the "lost people," the damned. We, like Percival, are the ones that Percy believes have sunk "so low."

Flannery O'Connor explains what this "low" place looks like to a Christian writer in the modern world: "The novelist with Christian concerns will find in modern life distortions which are repugnant to him, and his problem will be to make these appear as distortions to an audience which is used to seeing them as natural."[3] As a Christian novelist in twentieth-century America, Percy assumes the role of a modern Dante who must contrast the accepted norms of his society with a salvific vision. However, Percy agrees with O'Connor that such a vision seems impossible in his age. While crafting *Lancelot,* Percy laments to Shelby Foote, "I think what's got me down is that the novel is attempting the impossible: to write about the great traditional themes, sin, God, love, death, etc., when in fact these themes are no longer with us" (*Correspondence* 179).

While Percy originally intended to write the story from Percival's perspective, he discovered a direct approach was impossible. To vivify the dead ideas such as sin, God, and so on required an indirect approach. Percy must discuss the subjects inversely, through their opposites, so he depicts a man who does not believe in sin, who is demonic, and who confuses love with sex, and death with life. The epigraph to Camus's *The Fall* suits Lancelot as well: he is "the aggregate of the vices of our whole generation in their fullest expression."[4] In the aforementioned essay by O'Connor, she concludes with a quote from St. Cyril of Jerusalem: "We go to the Father of Souls, but it is necessary to pass by the dragon." She explains, "No matter what form the dragon may take, it is of the mysterious passage past him, or into his jaws, that stories of any depth will always be concerned to tell."[5] As Dante must climb past the voracious three-mouthed Satan, so readers, especially those who have lost their belief in the traditional themes, must venture into the head of

Lancelot. By bringing readers through the mind of a devil, Percy desires to show them the way out of the demonic and into purgatory.

Percy does not exclude himself from those who have sunk so low. When Percy began writing *Lancelot,* he admits to several friends, including Foote, that he was struggling with depression. He calls it *acedia,* after the early church father's description of the noonday demon: "I've been in a long spell of *acedia,* anomie and aridity in which, unlike the saints who write under the assault of devils, I simply get sleepy and doze off."[6] At this point in Percy's life, his first three novels had all been nominated for the National Book Award. His elder daughter was married with two sons. His younger daughter was soon to be married and attending college. His wife, Bunt, was content serving the community and volunteering for everything from local to international causes. From undergraduates, editors, critics, and TV personalities, Percy was receiving public attention and acclaim for his work. Yet, all the personal and public success seems to have caused the malaise that he warns against in his fiction.

Unable to craft a new story, Percy turned his attention to writing essays and teaching fiction instead. He agreed to compile his essays for publication in 1975 as *The Message in the Bottle.* In 1974, he taught a seminar on alienation in literature at Louisiana State University in Baton Rouge, returning in spring 1975 to teach creative writing to a few select students. This teaching stint affected *Lancelot* in several ways. The novels that he taught in his literature seminar, such as Dostoevsky's *Notes from the Underground* and Camus's *The Fall* and *The Stranger,* became models for creating Lancelot's character. Moreover, Percy read these authors' essays about their writing process and recommended these resources to his students. Both by teaching creative writing and by studying the writing process from Dostoevsky and Camus, Percy became hyperconscious of his storytelling techniques, which bears out in the metafictional approach in *Lancelot.* Finally, the setting of a college campus appears in cameo form, and the activities of 1970s college students, such as promiscuous sex and prevalent drug use, are laced throughout the story.

Lancelot is coarser and more violent than any of Percy's other novels.

Like *Love in the Ruins*, it experiments with genre and style, though this time with southern Gothic. Like one of Edgar Allan Poe's mystery stories, *Lancelot* is horrific, surreal, and full of murder and seduction. Whereas Tom More was doubtful as a trustworthy narrator, Lancelot is explicitly a liar. Moreover, he is a murderer and a prisoner in a Center for Aberrant Behavior; he is categorically insane. Percy continues his concerns from *Love in the Ruins* by pushing them to the extreme in *Lancelot*. We are now inside the head of the possessed, receiving firsthand knowledge of the demonic, and listening to someone who desires to end the world.

Lancelot is an idler, a disillusioned retired lawyer who used to fight for the NAACP until the drama of the 1960s civil rights movement gave way to the banality of the 1970s.[7] He resides on Belle Isle, a southern plantation reminiscent of the homes from *Gone With the Wind*, and profits from midwestern tourists in hoop skirts who "ooh" and "ahh" as his black servants offer spiels about the history of his mansion and its antique furniture. A widower, Lancelot marries one of these tourists, Margot Reilly, a wannabe actress from Texas, who remakes him in her image. To Margot, Lancelot becomes a composite of Leslie Howard as Ashley Wilkes, Gregory Peck (from *To Kill a Mockingbird*), Clark Gable as Rhett, and Jefferson Davis "home from the wars and set up in style by another strong-minded women at Beauvoir, parked out in a pigeonnier."[8] Instead of scribbling his memoirs in imitation of Davis, however, Lancelot spends most of his time in the pigeonnier drinking alcohol and watching the news. Lancelot foils the persona of the southern gentleman.

While Lancelot may be a convincing narrator, the reader should remember first that he is a liar and second that the "I" of the first person is not Percy. In a review in the *New York Times*, Christopher Lehmann-Haupt, for instance, assumes that Percy is his protagonist: "[I]f it is true that Lancelot Lamar is not Walker Percy, then it is one of the very few respects in which this novel works as fiction."[9] Because many of Lancelot's gripes match those of Percy, readers fail to distinguish the author from his character. However, the novel intends to instruct readers in how to practice such discernment. One must sift out the true from the false in Lancelot's narrative and see beneath the guises to locate the real.

Percy symbolically depicts this problem between make-believe and reality in the movie filmed in town and at the Belle Isle mansion. At the time when Percy was writing *Lancelot,* producer Kit Carson was attempting to film *The Moviegoer,* which may have inspired Percy. At the same time, all the headlines about the Manson murders (1969–72) of Hollywood celebrities may have contributed to this plot device.[10] In addition to muddying the waters of reality, the film contributes to false conceptions by exploiting caricatures of southern myths, such as a Cajun trapper, a sharecropper, and the decadent aristocratic southern gentleman. Moreover, the actors play parts both on and off the set. For instance, the famous beauty Raine Robinette, whom Lancelot compares to Ava Gardner, enjoys her role as a tease to Lancelot, as a sexual mentor to Lucy, and as a "down-to-earth" celebrity to the rest of the town (L 234, 111). Lancelot's wife, Margot, does not share Raine's acting abilities: when she is off camera, she acts, and when she is filming, she acts like an actress acting. Lancelot observes her on set one day: "What [Margot] was doing was not acting, that is, imitating someone else, but acting like an actress imitating-someone-else. She was once removed from the acting" (146). After Lancelot confronts her about her adultery, Margot can do little more than play a role. He notices that she acts like "Nora Helmer in *A Doll's House,*" the part she is leaving him to play in London (208). From Lancelot's perspective, everyone around him begins to act as though in the movies (200, 205).

Although all of the acting disgusts Lancelot, he becomes worse than all of the actors. He joins their industry by secretly filming their sexual escapades, reducing his fellow human beings not merely to actors but further to stick figures and lines in diagrams. He himself becomes an actor, reduced to playing a part. Before the final atrocious acts of the novel, Lancelot consumes a drug that sets distance between him and his self; he starts to watch himself as an actor in his life (208–9). When Lancelot sexually assaults Raine at the conclusion of the novel, for instance, he cannot understand why the experience does not live up to his locker-room fantasies: "Why is the real so different from the fantasy?" (234). As Lancelot has become disconnected from himself, the real feels more unreal to him than the fantasy.

In Lancelot's world, the real and the facade too easily assimilate. Lancelot considers himself the product of a charade. His father played the role of honorable southern gentleman, editor of a weekly newspaper, and local politician, but he had taken kickbacks from local agencies, which Lancelot discovered in his sock drawer. The illusion of his honorable family dissolves. In addition to the false front of his father, Lancelot's mother cuckolds her husband with Lancelot's Uncle Harry— an obvious allusion to Hamlet when Queen Gertrude foils her husband and marries his brother, Claudius. Even Lance's home, Belle Isle, is a pretense, a show of southern aristocracy that lacks the necessary funds for its upkeep. When Lancelot recalls his own fame for saving Elgin's family from the Klan, he separates the "slightly bogus" story from the true version (92). Lancelot reflects, "[I]n the grand mythic Lamar tradition I had confronted the Kleagle in his den, 'called him out' with some such Southern Western shoot-out ultimatum" (92). However, in reality, Lancelot simply asks the Grand Kleagle, "a big dumb boy" with whom he used to play football, to lay off his "niggers," and the two of them share a drink (93). For Lancelot, these memories are evidence that goodness is a front for the unseemly reality of things.

By addressing the discrepancies between the real and the false, Lance compels both Percival and the reader to decipher what is real and false in his narrative. At the start of their second meeting, Lancelot confesses to Percival, "I was not quite honest yesterday when I pretended not to know you. I knew you perfectly well" (9). His honesty about his previous dishonesty causes us to doubt his sincerity at other moments in the narrative. Knowing that Lance lies, Percival must question the veracity of his tale. As readers, we too have to consider what is true and false in Percy's story, what features of Lance's monologue correlate with reality, and which ones are the result of poor vision. Additionally, Lance calls out Percival as one who also has been guilty of playing a part. When they met for the first time as youths, Percival was reading Verlaine (much like Tom More was), and Lancelot asks him, "It was a bit of an act, wasn't it?" (13). Lancelot assumes that all people are actors putting on a front. This query may also be directed at the reader: do you put on an act, reader? "We are all unreliable narrators of our own lives," classicist James J. O'Donnell writes in his biography of St. Augustine.[11] The metafictional approach that Percy takes with *Lancelot* forces readers to confront not only the methods of Lance's storytelling but also the ways that we tell our own stories.

For Lancelot, the story begins with his discovery of his wife's infidelity. Stumbling upon his younger daughter Siobhan's blood type, Lancelot checks the potential dates of her conception and realizes that he could not have fathered her. Although the facts are irrefutable, Lancelot undertakes a quest for certainty of his wife's betrayal, a quest which includes voyeurism, spying on his wife, manipulating her and her coworkers, videotaping her with her lovers, and finally breaking into their bedroom and murdering them. Playing on the Arthurian source of his name, the knight Lancelot's search for the Holy Grail of Christ, Lancelot calls himself "The Knight of the Unholy Grail" and defines his investigation as a "quest for evil" (*L* 138). Such a search parodies the searches that Binx and Barrett undertake in Percy's first two novels. Although Lancelot is another "Robinson Crusoe," as his Percyean predecessors have been, he awakens not to the possibility of God but to the possibility of sin (140). As he informs Percival, "Good proves nothing. When everyone is wonderful, nobody bothers with God. [But] what if one should find the devil?" (138–39). So with different intentions from his author, Lancelot assumes a similar quest into the "darling heart of darkness" (208). When Lancelot reaches the "heart of evil," he encounters "nothing now except a certain coldness" (253). Theologically, Lancelot's finding correlates with Christian tradition: both St. Augustine and St. Aquinas argue that evil is the absence of being. As "cold" is the absence of heat or "darkness" the absence of light, Lancelot discovers that "evil" is the absence of good.

The catalyst for his quest is the sexual transgression of his wife. While probing into his wife's midnight affairs, Lancelot also uncovers his elder daughter's sexual promiscuity. She has been seduced by two of the actors in her stepmother's film. The problem, for Lancelot, is that sex seems to matter so little to people around him. He tells Percival that his son, who remains nameless, "appears to be a mild homosexual. But in either case, hetero or homo, it doesn't seem to count for a great deal to him" (17). Lancelot wonders why he is the only one "hung up" on the issue of sex (17). "Not even your church," Lancelot complains to Percival, indicting the Roman Catholic Church, "took it very seriously until recent years. Dante was downright indulgent with sexual sinners. They occupied a rather pleasant anteroom to hell" (17). In contrast to the Church, Dante, Lancelot's offspring, and his wife, Lance believes sex to be the objective of existence: "[T]he monstrous truth lying at the very center of life [is] that [women's] happiness and the meaning of life itself is to be assaulted by a man" (222). Going further than Descartes's reduction of human beings to thinking creatures, Lance reduces man to a "thinking reed and a walking genital" (223).

Lance's obsession with sex embodies the tenor of 1970s American culture: in 1972 the illustrated sex manual *The Joy of Sex* became a bestseller, and in 1973 the American Psychiatric Association removed homosexuality from its official list of mental disorders. These two events are small illustrations of the changes that affected Percy's interpretation of his culture's evolving perspective on sex. However, Percy's Catholic friends and reviewers could not understand the novel's exploitation of sex. When Brainard Cheney, for example, accused Percy of pornography, Percy defended *Lancelot*: "If you think I write pornography—as astute as you are . . . you may be right. . . . [However,] [p]ornography is scandal in my book."[12] In part, Percy intends to scandalize readers out of their complacency regarding sex. He seems to concur with his protagonist when he writes that, for "the present generation," sex "doesn't even seem to rate among the Top Ten experiences" (*L* 17). But, even more so, Percy is showcasing Lancelot as the pornographer; he is the scandalous one. Percy desires that his audience feel scandalized, but that they point their finger at the character and not the author.

O'Connor calls "pornography" one of the worst "sins of bad taste in fiction," the other being sentimentality. She defends the "scandal" of her stories to a Catholic editor as a way of showing a "whole view of things."[13] For O'Connor, the reason that pornography, and like it sentimentality, sin against fiction is because they mistake a partial view for the whole. Throughout *Lancelot*, the main character has been unable to grasp what sex is. He reduces it to "cells touching cells" (*L* 17) or "his wife's thighs spread, a cry, not recognizably hers, escaping her lips" (21). In both descriptions, Lancelot replaces the whole person—body and soul—with its parts. Moreover, he obsesses with sex to the point of videotaping his wife and her lovers as well as his daughter with her lovers. Sex becomes all-encompassing to Lancelot, the very purpose of his life. When O'Connor writes against pornography, she defends the use of sex to "prove your point" or "to further the story."[14] As an author, Percy confines his descriptions of sex to these parameters, but as a character and a narrator himself, Lancelot surpasses them. Lancelot is the pornographer.

For Lancelot, sex assumes religious significance and the potential for transcendence. He calls the gospel of life "pornography" (224), and he adopts religious language to describe sexual matters. When Lancelot creeps into his wife's bedroom to murder her and her lover, he describes their bed—his marriage bed—as an altar with a "flying buttress" (238). As he listens to the two commit adultery, Lancelot refers to himself as "an unconsecrated priest hearing an impenitent confession" in which their voices rise and fall "in prayer-like intonation. God. Sh—God. Sh—" (238). Whereas elsewhere, Lancelot curses without hesitation, he censors the lovers' exclamations and reflects, "Why not then curse and call on God in an act of love?" (238). Lancelot then rises above the lovers, describing them as a "beast," and descends upon them to smother them. Like an ancient priest sacrificing an animal on an altar, Lance clutches his wife's lover and slashes his throat.

Percy reveals that violence is the natural end of Lancelot's false vision, his reduction of human beings to objects, and of the world into either/or categories. When Lancelot initially speaks to Percival, he asks, "You like my little view. Have you noticed that the narrower the vision the more you can see?" (3). What is the answer to his rhetorical question? Is Lancelot right or wrong in this opening paragraph? The question highlights the significance of vision for the rest of the narrative. Lancelot's vision is impeded by his assumptions about reality: he casts human beings as sexual objects to be divided into genders, races, classes, and even good and bad.

According to Lancelot's system, men are made to assault women, and women are meant to be either whores or ladies. As Margot informs him minutes before she dies, "With you I had to be either—or—but never a—uh—woman" (245). Lancelot divides the women in his life into these categories: his first wife, Lucy, was a virgin and thus a lady, but Margot is an adulteress. He reflects, "I wanted Margot's sweet Texas ass and I wanted Lucy's opaque Georgia eyes" (85). Preceding his murder and arson, Lancelot is visited in his pigeonnier by an apparition of a woman who appears to muddle his division between whore and lady. He calls this phantom "Our Lady of the Camellias," which refers simultaneously to "Our Lady," the Virgin Mary, and to Alexander Dumas's novel *The Lady of the Camellias* about a courtesan and Dumas's real-life lover. Because Lancelot has consumed a drug, he cannot ascertain whether the vision is real or false, and for a moment, the woman reminds him of his deceased mother (*L* 212). The woman also assumes the role of the Arthurian Lady of the Lake who proffers Excalibur. In an ironic contrast, just as the Lady of the Lake grants the future king of the Britons the legendary sword, this phantom lady procures the Bowie knife with which Lance murders his wife's lover (226). When she holds the sword, Lancelot wonders whether she is imitating "Joan of Arc leading her army, cross borne aloft" (225). Although Lancelot has spent the novel dividing women into ladies or whores, this apparition, as both seductress and saint, confounds his categories.

The other woman who problematizes Lancelot's easy distinctions is the one residing in the hospital cell adjacent to his, Anna, who was gang-raped and has gone temporarily mute from the shock. "She is the first woman of the new order," Lancelot tells Percival. "For she has, so to speak, endured the worst of the age and survived it, undergone the ultimate violation and come out of it not only intact but somehow purged, innocent" (159). Because Anna has suffered the worst assault on her flesh, Lancelot views her as reborn. He insists that he is not joking: "Who else might the new Virgin be but a gang-raped social worker?" (159). Lancelot plans to marry her, but she refuses. When he explains his view of her, she is offended. She rejects his insinuations: "Are you suggesting [. . .] that I, myself, me, my person, can be violated by a *man?* [. . .] Don't you know that there are more important things in this world? Next you'll be telling me that despite myself I liked it" (251). She is right, of course. Lancelot not only assumes that the violation penetrated more than her flesh, but also that she probably enjoyed the assault (252). By exaggerating the importance of sex, Lancelot misconceives Anna's situation. Not to mention, his reductionist view of women as either ladies or whores blinds him to Anna as a person apart from her sexual status.

The "new order" that Lancelot mentions to Percival, in which he dreams Anna will be the "first woman," is a "Third Revolution," a horrifying scheme for the future that outdoes the vision of Dostoevsky's Grand Inquisitor from *The Brothers Karamazov*. Several critics have drawn connections between Dostoevsky's Grand Inquisitor and Lancelot, including Linda Whitney Hobson, John Desmond, and myself in another book.[15] "The Legend of the Grand Inquisitor" is a poem penned by Dostoevsky's character Ivan Karamazov, an unacknowledged atheist. In this piece, a fifteenth-century Spanish inquisitor explains to a returned Christ why the world does not need a divine superhero. Instead of the Son of God who promises forgiveness for sins and eternal life, the Grand Inquisitor steps forward to provide for the here and now with earthly sustenance. He offers people bread and entertainment, as well as authority. Recognizing that people cannot handle the freedom that God gives them, the inquisitor removes it and becomes their authoritarian provider. Dostoevsky highlights the violence of such a vision. When Christ first enters the scene, the inquisitor is overseeing the burning of a hundred so-called heretics. While the inquisitor determines to correct Christ's work by seeing to the material needs of the church, he does so at the cost of life.

Lancelot unknowingly emulates the Grand Inquisitor's vision. He encounters the truth of the inquisitor's claims, an "incidental discovery" to his discovery of sexual sin: "If you tell somebody what to do, they will do it. All you have to do is know what to do. Because nobody else does" (*L* 196).[16] Like the inquisitor, Lance replaces authority with authoritarianism. He removes others' freedom, objectifies everyone, and determines to establish a new order, regardless of whether millions must die for its formation. Lancelot compares his "Third Revolution" to the first two revolutions in America (the Revolutionary War and the Civil War). Whereas he views the first as successful, the second failed because the South lost (157). His Third Revolution will succeed. He casts his lot with those "Christians" who believe "in a God who said he came not to bring peace but the sword" (157). While Lancelot protests that his revolution should not be confused with the Klan or the Nazis or other political organizations, it sounds uncomfortably similar (156). Fed up with "this age," Lancelot determines to undergo a crusade for honor. He sounds a lot like a perverse Aunt Emily when he calls himself the "last of the West" and the "best of" everyone (178). One may hear a parody of Percy's Uncle Will's *Lanterns on the Levee*, for which Percy had recently written an introduction in 1975. This new order is southern Stoicism regained with the aid of a sword, or, in Lance's case, a Bowie knife.

As the founding member of his revolution, Lance proposes to become the new arbiter between the good and the bad. From his perspective, the "great whorehouse and fagdom of America" cannot continue (*L* 176). Lancelot tells Percival, "We are living in Sodom" (255). And, like God, Lancelot proposes to destroy the age with his own versions of fire and brimstone. In the 1990s, philosopher Peter Kreeft joked, "[I]f God spares New York, he will owe an apology to Sodom."[17] Yet, God seems, to Lancelot, to tolerate the immorality of American cities; Lancelot uses the seeming idleness of God as evidence against God's existence. As Lancelot sees it, if God existed, he would end this age. However, because God seems powerless to stop the sexual degradation in his world, Lancelot claims, like Dostoevsky's Grand Inquisitor, a godlike role in determining to "start a new world singlehandedly" with the sword, if that's what it takes (*L* 256).

Lancelot must incite a "Third Revolution" because Percival's God and his Catholic Church have failed. Just as the Grand Inquisitor has found Christ useless for worldly purposes, so Lancelot casts out Christ as ineffectual, emasculated, and nothing but an empty cipher. When Lancelot refers to Christ or God purposefully, he uses the possessive pronoun "your" as a modifier, to distinguish between his atheism and Percival's Catholicism. First, this God failed because his Church does not categorically denounce certain actions, such as sex. Lancelot complains that the Church's rules on sex are too muddled: "You want to have it both ways: good, but—bad only if—and so forth" (176). When Lancelot uses "You" here, he refers not only to Percival but also to "God" and "Christ" as well. Several times he refers to Percival as "Christ" or "Jesus," though the epithets are unintentional. While the "old Catholic way" may have been tenable at one time, the Catholics blew it with their "God-bless-everything-because-it's-good-only-don't-but-if-you-do-it's-not-so-bad" (177). Lancelot prefers his dichotomous absolutes; he adheres to his either/or way of seeing the world. To Lancelot's mind, the Christ of the Gospels who chose "peace" and "love" too easily permitted sexual perversion. Because of what Lancelot perceives as Christ's lackadaisical attitude to fornication, the world has become Sodom. Lancelot assumes that Christ—by being as silent as Percival—is inactive in the world, and thus fallaciously concludes that Christ tolerates this age.

By attempting to replace Christ and by setting himself as the standard and arbiter of the good (which, for him, is evil), Lancelot imitates the fallen angel Lucifer. He is a parody of Christ and offers a satanic alternative to Percival's Catholicism. At the end of the novel, Lancelot proposes that there are only two ways, either his way or Percival's: "There is no other way than yours or mine, true?" to which his previously silent interlocutor responds, "Yes" (257). Because only Lancelot and Percival in the Arthurian legends found the Grail, it is fitting that they possess the two potential exits out of this current intolerable age (176). Percy equates Lancelot's plan with the demonic, alluding to Lancelot as "Satan" (254) and "Lucifer" (246). Percy ties Lancelot to Dante's version of the demon by giving him "great wings" (246). In Dante's *Inferno*, Satan has six wings all beating incessantly and keeping him frozen in the center of hell.

Dante's *Inferno* provides another hint to Lancelot's demonic identity: his inability to reside in the present. In Dante's hell, the eternally damned sinners can only remember their past and see forward to the future, but they are blind to the current state of the world. Nearly all of them question Dante the pilgrim regarding contemporary affairs because they have no knowledge of them. The Christian apologist, novelist, and medieval scholar C. S. Lewis stole this attribute when he created his devil, Screwtape, who writes letters to a young demon-in-training, Wormwood.[18] Lewis's *The Screwtape Letters* was published in 1942, and Percy may have read it because we know he read much of Lewis's other works.[19] In it the devil advises his trainee to convince the patient, the potential sinner, "to live in the Past." But then Screwtape has misgivings about this advice: "But this is of limited value, for [humans] have some real knowledge of the past and it has a determinate nature and, to that extent, resembles eternity. It is far better to make them live in the Future." While Screwtape's enemy, God, desires his people to live in the present moments, the devil knows that "nearly all vices are rooted in the future."[20] With its lack of concrete existence, the future becomes the realm of the demonic, which is a place of endless deferral.

Lancelot feels most comfortable in the future, again betraying his true nature. When Percy first created the character, he made Lancelot an amnesic: "What he does not know, and has made himself forget, and pieces together later, is that he has killed his wife" (*Correspondence* 153). In the published version, Lancelot does not forget but feigns forgetfulness because the past is not worth remembering. "It was as if," Lancelot confesses, "I didn't have the—the what?—the inclination to think about the past" (*L* 13). Since the beginning of his story, Lancelot has hesitated to speak about what happened, not from remorse or guilt but from apathy. Lancelot claims, "The past devours the future like a tape recorder, converting pure possibility into banality. The present is the tape head, the mouth of time" (106). For Lancelot, only the "pure possibility" inspires his "worm of interest" (21). If Lewis is correct, the present shares too much with God's perspective: "For the Present is the point at which time touches eternity."[21] Lancelot rejects the present, perhaps for this reason. "To live in the past and future is easy," he tells Percival, "[But to] live in the present is like threading the needle" (*L* 235). He prefers to slide back and forth between the present and future, focusing primarily on his diabolical revolution.

In contrast to Lancelot's way, Percival presents a return to the "Little Way" that Tom More chose at the conclusion of *Love in the Ruins*. As a priest, Father John will "take a little church in Alabama" where he will "preach the gospel, turn bread into flesh, forgive the sins of Buick dealers, administer communion to suburban housewives," and thus live the sacramental life (*L* 256). Although Percival never describes his way, we have heard some of it explained—though inversely—from Lancelot. Percival responds with twelve "Yeses" and one "No" to Lancelot's final questions about what will happen next. Again, the numerology so significant in Dante may have compelled Percy to use a similar device. The twelve affirmations suggest the biblical twelve disciples or Israel's tribes against the one demonic negative. In addition to the simple numbers game, the end promises hope by offering the last word to Percival. When Lancelot asks, "Is there anything you wish to tell me before I leave?" Percival answers, "Yes" (257). The reader has been waiting for him to speak during the whole novel. Although we do not hear what Percival says, we can assume it will be the good news. Whether Lancelot will reject or accept Percival's preaching is another story.[22]

While it may be easy to overlook Percival in *Lancelot* because of his silence, his presence is vital to comprehending the meaning of the text. Lancelot himself recognizes that his story will not exist without Percival's presence; as he insists, "I sense there is a clue I've missed and that you might pick it up. It is as if I knew that the clue was buried somewhere in the rubble of Belle Isle and that I have to spend days kicking through the ashes to find it. . . . I couldn't do that alone. But we could do it" (106). In order to remember what has happened, Lancelot claims that he needs another person with whom to dialogue, and not just any person, but specifically Percival. Farrell O'Gorman notes that as a doctor and priest, an authority on both the body and soul, Percival provides a strong contrast to Lancelot's abstract theorizing.[23] Moreover, as a childhood friend and fraternity brother, only Percival shares "a kinship of spirit" and reflects Lancelot's self to him (*L* 5).

Although Lancelot defines himself in opposition to Percival (as the demonic might do against the divine), both are able to see that something has gone wrong in the world. Lancelot senses immediately that "something went wrong with [Percival] too" (11). When Lancelot asks whether the way of the world must end and the new begin, Percival assents. In response to the way of Raine, Jacoby, and Margot, and even Lance's children, Percival has gone silent and Lance has gone mad. They denounce the "middle way" outside the prison as the "relativistic, aesthetical world, symbolized by Hollywood," as Linda Whitney Hobson describes it.[24] Both have seen the heart of evil: Lance, through firsthand experience, and Percival, through Lance's story.

As readers, we too have experienced some of this evil heart. This book is tremendously difficult to read. While as comic as Percy's previous novels, its comedy is not light and easy. After the success of Lewis's diabolic novel, *The Screwtape Letters*, his fans cried out for a sequel, which Lewis set himself against. Writing in the voice of the demonic "almost smothered" him, and Lewis asserts, "It would have smothered my readers if I had prolonged it."[25] So, too do we experience such smothering from Percy's diabolical narrator. The purpose of venturing into this evil heart is that readers may, with greater awareness of the demonic nature of the alternative, choose between the revolution of Lancelot or the little way of Percival.

Percy explains in his interviews that he does not allow Percival to reply fully to Lancelot's harangue because the "esthetic limitations of the novel-form" (*More Conversations* 146). What Percy means alludes to Kierkegaard's essay "Of the Difference between a Genius and an Apostle." For Percy, the novelist does not have the authority to dictate the good news, but Percival, as a priest, does possess that authority. As a novelist, Percy's goal is to make readers aware that something is wrong with the world, which *Lancelot* does more than adequately. However, the silence of Percival accomplishes more than Percy intended. Imitating the silence of Christ in "The Legend of the Grand Inquisitor" and of Alyosha Karamazov who listens to Ivan's poem, Percival exhibits an answer to Lancelot's tirade.

Percival's silence is not due to an inability to talk or the lack of something to say. When Percival first enters Lance's cell, he opens his mouth to speak, but then chooses silence as the best response (*L* 4). His silence encourages Lancelot to speak. Lancelot explains, "[W]hat first struck me about you was that you're the only person around here who doesn't want to talk" (5). Although the doctors, psychiatrists, and priests have prattled at him constantly, Lancelot has refused to speak to any of them and is "certainly not interested in what they say" (5). Instead of arguing with Lancelot, Percival offers his attention. French philosopher Simone Weil contends that such attention exhibits genuine love for other people: "The soul empties itself of all its own contents in order to receive into itself the being it is looking at, just as he is, in all his truth."[26] Percival's attention counteracts Lance's case for classifying people into categories and reducing them to objects. It is the best refutation that he could offer.

As a novel, then, *Lancelot* only postures as pornography and demonic heyday. Alyosha Karamazov's response to Ivan's Grand Inquisitor poem may be the reader's response to Percy's novel: "Your [work] praises Jesus, it doesn't revile him. . . ."[27] When readers feel scandalized by Lancelot's language or his lewd portrayals of sex, they are rebutting Lancelot's conclusion that "the only emotion people feel nowadays is interest or the lack of it" (*L* 21). If Percy has inspired horror in his reader, then Lancelot is wrong. People do still have feelings, commit sins, make confession, and hope for redemption. They fall in love and care for their children and take communion in small southern churches. Although Percy did not live to read it, what Pope John Paul II writes in his "Letter to Artists" (1999) applies well to Percy's novel: "Even when they explore the darkest depths of the soul or the most unsettling aspects of evil, artists give voice in a way to the universal desire for redemption." The long-winded, startling voice of Lancelot has not sucked all of the air out of the room. If Pope John Paul II is correct, then, in a paradoxical twist, Lancelot's voice has shed more light than darkness.

5
The Second Coming

The Second Coming (1980) begins with a man on a golf course who realizes that "something ha[s] gone wrong" (3). Like Percy's previous castaways, this man awakens to despair and considers the possibility "that he might shoot himself" (4). Percy seems to be returning to old themes, and, as further evidence of repetition, the man himself is named Will Barrett, the hero from *The Last Gentleman*. At the conclusion of *The Last Gentleman*, Barrett declared to Sutter Vaught, "It is better to do something than nothing; it is good to have a family; it is better to love and be loved. . . . I think I see for the first time the possibility of a happy, useful life" (*LG* 385). Now, at the start of *The Second Coming*, Barrett can say he has "succeeded in his life in every way one can imagine" (*SC* 9). He has met all of the goals that he set for a successful life, yet something is missing. This is a different Will Barrett from the one we have previously known. Rather than a young amnesiac unsure of his place in the world, this Barrett is a middle-aged retired widower who remembers everything. The former declarations of the young Will Barrett have proven a weak formula for the good life, and the search is on again for something more than what this world has offered.

One key difference between this novel and Percy's previous stories is the addition of a female heroine. While the concluding marriages in Percy's other novels—Binx and Kitty or Tom and Ellen—are treated like byproducts of the search, in *The Second Coming*, *eros* battles *thanatos* at the center of the plot, and the consummate romance between Will and Allie Huger is the only possible happy ending for the story. Allie contrasts with Barrett for much of the novel, and eventually becomes his complement. In every way, Allie's condition counters Barrett's predicament: she has failed in life, and she remembers nothing. She is a young schizophrenic, recently escaped from an asylum, seeking refuge in a greenhouse and discovering a talent for "hoisting." He is an older man, well respected in the community, who has begun suffering from falling episodes. The novel jumps between their perspectives until the two points of view become intertwined at the novel's end.

After the dark satire of *Lancelot*, the romance of Percy's fifth novel is a gift of light. Despite the publisher's high hopes for *Lancelot*, the book never gained traction. "How could it?" Percy wondered, "[It is] a dramatic monologue—a basically uncongenial form—the reader still likes a once-upon-a-time third-person-singular story and he may be right" (*Correspondence* 238). While *The Second Coming* provides the reader with such a story in a fable-like romance, the ideas that undergird *Lancelot* are not forgotten. John Desmond notes, "Almost everything we see in this representative fictive world—its hypocrisy, its vapid pietistic language, its conformity and devaluation of the inner quest for faith—seems to justify Lancelot Lamar's angry attacks on society in *Lancelot*."[1] Whereas *Lancelot* attempted to denounce these evils by exposing their dark extremes, *The Second Coming* offers Percival's way. It shows the third way of ordinary life, which Barrett and Allie will find in one another, and eventually in the Roman Catholic Church.

In *The Second Coming*, Percy symbolizes the life of the "little way" in "buried treasure" (61). While watching *King Solomon's Mines* (1950)—an adventure film that invokes again the theme of treasure hunting—Barrett ponders, "Was there a whole world of meaning, of talking and listening, which took place everywhere and all the time which no one paid attention to, at least not he?" (*SC* 325). Over the course of the novel, Barrett discovers that words, as well as things all around him, are signs to be attended to. In the biblical book of Isaiah, the prophet takes on God's voice and writes, "I will give you hidden treasures, riches stored in secret places, so that you may know that I am the Lord."[2] Allie and Barrett find that the world is a treasure map of sorts with signs indicating where to go and what one will discover at the end of the journey.

When Allie initially escapes the asylum, she carries a set of instructions with her, notes from herself "on how to locate the house, things to buy, and so forth," which a stranger calls "a treasure hunt" (36). She repeats the phrase "treasure hunt" as an apt metaphor for her undertaking. Moreover, Allie remembers that her "Aunt Sally" called the island that she bequeaths Allie "worthless unless the treasure Captain Kidd was supposed to have buried there was ever dug up" (39). This idea of treasure dominates Allie's consciousness: "It wasn't even the treasure I liked," she thinks, "but the island and the idea of something being hidden there and finding it" (120). This symbol resurfaces numerous times in how Allie views her new adventure at the greenhouse, part of her inheritance, discovering the "treasure" of a stove in the ground (92) and comparing the cellar of her new dwelling to King Tut's tomb, where "some few treasures" are stored (82). The meaning of this symbol is further unveiled as Allie reads the book she finds at the greenhouse, *Captain Blood*, a book about treasure hunting. Meditating on a passage from the text, she concludes, "Words surely have meanings" (*SC* 82). For the reader, a treasure map has been drawn with clues in the metaphor of "treasure" itself and the meaning of language. In part, the treasure may not be found without knowing the meaning of words.

Barrett stumbles upon this problem while playing golf and remembering a hunting trip with his father in the Georgia swamp. He recalls a piece of the memory that had until this moment remained dormant. His father had tried to kill him. To this discovery, Barrett responds, "Ah, I've found it after all. The buried treasure" (61). For Barrett, this buried treasure is "a secret" that his father "was trying to tell" him (62), a secret about life and death for which there are no meaningful words. "[T]here are worse things than death," his father tried to explain (126). "There is no word for it. What is the word for a state which is not life and not death, a death in life?" (126). The secret of life and death, for Barrett's father, is ineffable. Barrett's father recalls those in the Bible "who long for death that does not come, who search for it more than hidden treasure."³ In contrast to this longing for death, Barrett discovers a buried treasure, life itself.

In his essay "The Message in the Bottle," Percy uses the metaphor of buried treasure to refer to worn-out vocabulary. He writes, "The Christian novelist nowadays is like a man who finds a treasure buried in a field and sells all he has to buy the field, only to discover that everyone else has the same treasure in his field and that in any case real estate values have gone so high that all field-owners have forgotten the treasure and plan to subdivide" (117). Unlike the treasure in Jesus's parable (Matthew 13:44) likened to the "kingdom of heaven," the novelist's treasure has been devalued by his readers. "The old words of grace are worn smooth as poker chips and a certain devaluation has occurred," Percy claims (116). The news about the Christian gospel and its application to everyday life has become meaningless in a society where, as Binx Bolling puts it in *The Moviegoer*, "ninety-eight percent [of men] believe in God, and men are dead, dead, dead" (*MG* 228). How then to find the treasure of the "little way" if communicating about it has become void?

For the Christian novelist, such as Percy, the problem is how to deliver the news to his main characters in words that are meaningful and in a way that the castaways who receive the news will find relevant. In "The Message in the Bottle," Percy considers this dilemma by dissecting the situation between the good news, its deliverer, and its recipient. Percy describes a castaway in a desert approached by a man who claims to know what he needs. If the man, the newsbearer, claims that the castaway needs diamonds, then Percy asserts that he must be rejected for the ridiculousness of his proposition and its potential fraudulence. However, if instead he announces, "'Come! I know your need. I will take you to water'—then this very announcement is an earnest of his reliability" (*MIB* 134).

In *The Last Gentleman*, Barrett was a castaway who needed water. However, no one offered it to him. Val Vaught received such good news. When a stranger proposed that she was half-dead and offered, "[C]ome with me" to be alive (*LG* 300), Val followed and became a nun. Jamie Vaught receives the same good news from Father Boomer. However, Barrett requests the good news from the wrong newsbearer. He chooses Sutter as his apostle, a man who lacks reliable or authoritative news. Although Sutter continually rejects Barrett's requests for advice, Barrett attends to his messages. To use Percy's metaphor from *The Message in the Bottle*, Barrett chooses diamonds over water. The novel ends with Barrett standing in a desert and not receiving news but claiming that he needs Sutter. Thus, Percy writes *The Second Coming* about Barrett's second "come-ing," his second chance to hear good news and act on it.

At the start of *The Second Coming*, Barrett resembles the castaway from the movies that Binx Bolling used to watch. In *The Moviegoer* Binx laments that the movies screw up the search because the castaway "takes up with the local librarian, sets about proving to the local children what a nice fellow he is, and settles down with a vengeance. In two weeks' time he is so sunk in everydayness that he might just as well be dead" (13). Percy returns to this problem in "The Message in the Bottle": a castaway has lost his memory and awakens on a beach. "Being a resourceful fellow, he makes the best of a situation, gets a job, builds a house, takes a wife, raises a family, goes to night school, and enjoys the local arts of cinema, music, and literature. He becomes, as the phrase goes, a useful member of the community" (*MIB* 119). However, the problem is despair, an unawareness that the life one is living is actually death.

Percy has been observing this life-in-death phenomenon since his first novel. In *The Moviegoer*, Binx notices that, when he converses with people like the Lovells, they seem dead. He concludes, it is the death of scientific humanism "where needs are satisfied, everyone becomes an anyone [. . .] and men are dead, dead, dead" (228). Such observations remain consistent throughout Percy's novels. In *Love in the Ruins*, Father Smith describes the situation to Dr. Max Gottlieb: "I am surrounded by the corpses of souls. We live in a city of the dead" (186). While Gottlieb assumes these are the delusions of a madman, Tom More understands exactly what the priest means. And, Lancelot, as is his forte, puts the observations into an either/or dilemma: "Most people will die or exist as the living dead" (*L* 36). This either/or becomes Barrett's conclusion in *The Second Coming*. In fact, the only hero who seems not to observe the living dead is Will Barrett in *The Last Gentleman*. Although Barrett does observe that people appreciate life more in the midst of near-death experience, he never explicitly references the possibility of living as though dead.

When *The Last Gentleman* ends, Barrett assumes that physical death is the enemy, without any awareness of life-in-death as a potential problem. All that he has observed in the passing of Jamie is empirical death. He missed the sacramental nature of baptism that Father Boomer conducted and its corresponding hope for resurrection. To defeat physical death, Barrett halts Sutter's Edsel and postpones his friend's suicide—permanently postponed, as we discover in *The Second Coming*. After *The Last Gentleman* closes, Barrett pursues what he hopes is a good and successful life to the fullest. Yet, *The Second Coming* opens with Barrett "feeling depressed without knowing why. In fact, he didn't even realize he was depressed" (3). It is the character of despair, as Kierkegaard describes it, to be "unaware of being in despair." Only once Barrett realizes something is wrong can he begin confronting the despair and overcoming death-in-life.

The impetus that shakes Barrett into recognizing his despair is his memory of his father's attempt to kill him. Barrett calls this memory "the most important event in his life," one that he had until recently managed to forget (*SC* 3). Once he has remembered, Barrett spends much of the novel in dialogue with his father, whose ghost haunts the text as much as "King Hamlet's voice under the stage forces young Hamlet to 'swear' to avenge his murder," as Linda Whitney Hobson notes.[4] Barrett even refers to this voice as "old mole," the same name Hamlet uses to refer to his father. Until now, Barrett had forgotten the secret of life that his father tried to bestow on him. For his father, this secret was an either/or choice between death-in-life and death.

Like a less maniacal Lancelot, Barrett speculates about the nature of these two alternatives. He concludes that those who suffer living-death are the believers who, "like the Christians or Californians," believe everything, whereas the suicides are "the professors and scientists" and men like his father who believe in nothing (*SC* 190). The believers disguise death with belief. In his catalog of believers, Barrett includes his deceased wife, Marion, an "old-style Episcopalian who believed that one's duty lay with God, church, the *Book of Common Prayer*, family, country, and doing good works"; his daughter Leslie, "a new-style Christian who believed in giving her life to the Lord through a personal encounter with Him and who accordingly had no use of church, priests, or ritual"; Jack Curl, the pastor/handyman who seems most readily to believe in himself and his own causes; Kitty Vaught Huger, who follows astrology and professes reincarnation; and his servant Yamaiuchi, who is a Jehovah's Witness (158). On the other side, in league with his father, are those empiricist materialists who believe in nothing. They love death "because real death is better than the living death" (271).

After listing the variety of believers that surround him, Barrett wonders, "Is this an age of belief . . . a great renaissance of faith after a period of crass materialism, atheism, agnosticism, liberalism, scientism? Or is it an age of madness in which everyone believes everything? Which?" (159). This litany illustrates philosopher Charles Taylor's definition of a "secular age" in which "faith, even for the staunchest believer, is one human possibility among others."[5] It is an age of relativism and consumerism, even in regards to belief. Faith in God is one option equal with contending alternatives of belief.

In opposition to this false either/or, Barrett sets out on a quest to find a third way. Although Barrett's father categorized all contending options to death as death-in-life, Barrett asks, "Ah, but what if there is another way?" He determines, "I'm going to find out once and for all" (*SC* 132). In response to his father's proposition, Barrett proposes a search for what makes life worth living. In *The Last Gentleman*, the third way was Val and Father Boomer's Catholicism, although Barrett failed to recognize it as such. Catholicism, in Percy's work, is the real faith, and Catholics are those who believe not in everything or in nothing but in a few necessary things, those doctrines that Father Boomer lists at the conclusion of *The Last Gentleman*, such as the existence of God and the resurrection of Jesus Christ. Barrett realizes that he has "succeeded in everything except believing in the Christian God" (*SC* 73).

Barrett wonders whether belief in the Christian God is the only antidote to zombie-like living. Unfortunately, the Christians around him provide the greatest evidence against this belief. Barrett lives "in the most Christian nation in the world, the U.S.A., in the most Christian part of the nation, the South, in the most Christian state in the South, North Carolina, in the most Christian town in North Carolina," yet he thinks the Christians are the ones who have most missed it (13). "If the good news is true," Barrett wonders, "why is not one pleased to hear it? And if the good news is true, why are its public proclaimers such assholes and the proclamation itself such a weary used-up thing?" (189).

To determine whether Christianity is true, in spite of the hypocritical Christians around him, Barrett undertakes a quest more radical than any of Percy's previous heroes have dared.

Before his wife's death, Barrett waged nothing, attended church, and faked his Episcopalianism thoughtlessly. "Wasn't it possible to believe in God like Pascal's cold-blooded bettor, because there was everything to gain if you were right and nothing to lose if you were wrong?" (156). However, the problem with his previous Pascalian wager is that it cost nothing. Now, when Barrett makes a bet on God's existence, he stakes his own life. Barrett plans to enter an underground cave (where years ago his friend found the fossil of a saber-tooth tiger) and wait for a sign from God. If God refuses to grant him a sign, he will die. However, if God does exist, Barrett resolves to share the evidence with Sutter to publish in a scientific journal of his choice. Here, Barrett sounds truly mad. The existence of God should demand a change in his entire mode of being, but Barrett offers it only a footnote in academic literature.

To legitimize his lunatic treasure hunt for the Divine, Barrett compares himself to the biblical Jacob, who "require[d] an answer of God by hanging on to him" (193). Like the Old Testament Jew, Barrett wants to wrestle a blessing from God. For Barrett, it is the blessing of absolute, indisputable knowledge of God's existence. In *The Last Gentleman*, Barrett resembled Flannery O'Connor's "The Misfit" in her story "A Good Man Is Hard to Find," a serial killer who passed through a series of occupations without finding any meaning in life. In *The Second Coming*, Barrett echoes The Misfit, who cannot believe in Jesus because he did not witness the events of the Gospels. With cracked voice and tears in his eyes, The Misfit laments, "[I]f I had of been there I would of known and I wouldn't be like I am now" (*Collected Works* 152). Only firsthand experience warrants authority for The Misfit, and likewise for Barrett.

So the question is whether Barrett's plan is commendable. On the one hand, Barrett seems admirable because he refuses to accept the either/or dichotomy placed before him. In support of his scheme, he lists the biblical precedent of Jacob. In the Judeo-Christian tradition, he has further predecessors whom he neglects to mention. The prophet Elijah escaped to a cave to wait on God's voice, and God spoke to him there.

Before beginning his ministry, Jesus goes to a "desert place" to wait for the Spirit. And, there are many examples of ascetic monks and desert hermits living in caves, such as St. Anthony, who retreated there specifically to be with God. However, Barrett's desire to visit the "tyger" refers to the British poet William Blake and plays off "Blakean exploration of mythic depths," recalling the last gentleman's former romanticism (*SC* 183–84). Also, his decision to cart drugs, Placidyl tranquilizers, taints any potentially saintly motive. Finally, the poor craftsmanship of Barrett's letter to Sutter casts his proposal in a dubious light. The way that Barrett rambles on monologically for nearly a dozen pages sounds reminiscent of Lancelot. By assuming that he knows how Sutter will respond to the letter, Barrett removes all personhood from his friend and any possibility of real dialogue. Whatever the validity of the experiment, when Barrett describes it he sounds like a villain in a poorly written television show detailing his evil plan. Even the narrator calls his scheme a "peculiar delusion," and concludes, "So it was that Will Barrett went mad" (197).

Ironically, Barrett's plan for a third way hinges on an either/or dichotomy, and thus seems doomed to fail. The experiment does not go as Barrett intended. Although Barrett offers God an either/or choice, he neither receives a sign from God nor does he die. Or, if it is a sign from God, it is an indirect and oblique one too easily misconstrued: Barrett suffers from an abscessed tooth. The toothache causes so much pain that Barrett vomits and begins searching for an exit from the cave and his mad experiment. "There is one sure cure for cosmic explorations, grandiose ideas about God, man, death, suicide, and such," the narrator asserts, "—and that is nausea" (213). The physical reality of the nausea convicts Barrett to surrender his quest for metaphysical certainty about the existence of God. Gary Ciuba relates this scene to Jean-Paul Sartre's novel *Nausea*, in which the main character, Antoine Roquentin, suffers existential angst over the meaninglessness of life. Ciuba points out that "Will's nausea is not Roquentin's sickened response to the horrors of existence but a violent and physical corrective to an existence that has become too abstracted."[6] In opposition to Roquentin, who is nauseated by his abstraction, Barrett becomes less abstracted, more physically involved, through his nausea.

Attempting to extricate himself from his predicament, Barrett loses his way out of the cave only to fall headfirst through the ceiling of Allie's greenhouse. This fall, though brief, becomes the most significant of all his falls in the novel. Whereas his first fall, on the golf course, indicated that something had gone wrong, this fall introduces Barrett to something—or someone—right: Allie. In Percy's novels, vines symbolize apocalypse because the disorderly plant sprouts up and over the ordered, civilized world. However, the vines covering the hole to Allie's greenhouse are rotting away, and Barrett leaves the vines behind as he falls. Thus, the moment portends the end of Barrett's apocalyptic concerns. Moreover, "the great black beast of the apocalypse roaring down at him" fails to swallow him (*SC* 226). Instead, the stained glass that breaks beneath him resembles a "tacky heaven" (226). In this one fall, the supernatural seems to war over Barrett's perspective. One may imagine the scenes from Dante in which demons and angels battle over souls.[7] Barrett blacks out before knowing what has happened to him.

Percy asserted in "The Message in the Bottle" that the one who offers water to a castaway becomes a reliable source of news (*MIB* 134). When Barrett wakes, Allie is offering him a cup of water. The water quenches Barrett's extreme thirst; Allie meets Barrett's needs. After drinking the water, Barrett observes his surroundings and the stained-glass window through which he fell. "I'm in church," he concludes (*SC* 227). This inference foreshadows the connections that Barrett will make at the end of the novel between Allie's love and that of God. Furthermore, the greenhouse setting contrasts starkly with the barrenness of the cave. For Barrett, the cave symbolized death, haunted by the ghost of the tiger and the voice of his father. He intended it to be his burial place. In the cave, Barrett starved, grew thin, and went crazy under the sway of the Placidyl. Because of his abscessed tooth, the cave also became the location of sickness and fear. There, he was utterly isolated and in darkness. From this infernal locale, Barrett falls into a place of growth, where his thirst can be quenched, his hunger satisfied, and his body healed. Percy claims the greenhouse "was a very good symbol because it was unconscious" (*More Conversations* 51). In this "tacky" paradise, Barrett recovers himself, and, as he has been bathed by Allie, so he is symbolically reborn.

The Second Coming is filled with these metaphors. According to one reviewer, the novel contains "enough archetypal symbolism and mythopoetic incident to employ a busy Jungian researcher a decade."[8] Like the buried-treasure trope, the symbols of the cave, greenhouse, water, and others signify deeper meaning. One can imagine the cave as an allusion to Plato's *Republic*, and Barrett comes out to discover that he has been living in the shadows. It is as though Percy is teaching the reader to look for signs in the same way that Barrett himself is seeking after them.

For Barrett, the Jews are a sign, not only that something has gone wrong but also of the second coming of Christ. He questions Jack Curl about his wife's theory on the Jews: "Marion thought the Jews, the strange history of the Jews, were a sign of God's existence. What do you think?" (*SC* 136) Marion echoes Karl Barth's sentiment that the Jews are the best "proof of God . . . something visible and tangible, that no one could contest."[9] After all, they are an ancient group that has survived millennia. Of course, Barth made this statement standing at the ruins of Bonn University in 1946, after Hitler had decimated millions of Jews across Europe. If Barrett's ramblings about the Jews sound crazy, it is a holy foolishness supported by Barth and Percy, not to mention every other Percy hero or antihero who considered the Jews such a sign.

The whole novel is an exercise in reading the signs, of which Allie becomes, for Barrett, the primary sign of God. Allie and Will first meet on the golf green, or rather, off the green, as Will has sliced a ball far out of bounds. The ball crashes through her greenhouse window and disturbs her, as she lies reading *Captain Blood*. When Will first speaks with Allie, he cannot figure her out. As Val confounded him in *The Last Gentleman*, so Allie does in *The Second Coming*. He gauges her strange clothes, vintage haircut, and slow, measured way of speaking, not to mention the eccentric vocabulary. While Allie seems "as familiar to him as he himself" (*SC* 77), Barrett disengages from the conversation. Rather than investigate her identity or circumstance, he assumes she is on drugs. This conclusion allows him to walk away unfazed and uninvolved, though still simmering from some unacknowledged "anger" for which he cannot locate a source (75). In contrast to Allie's calm acceptance of their encounter, Barrett's stewing anger suggests that more is wrong with him than with her.

Up to this moment, Allie has been attempting to put together the pieces of a life. Her parents have treated her like an inconvenience and planned for her future based on their own best interests. However, one day, Allie decides "for the first time in her life: What if *I* make the plans for me?" (105). This moment initiates a claim of her selfhood, a discovery of the "I-I" (105). Allie plans to flee the hospital and its electroshock treatments, locate her inherited property, and establish a home in the greenhouse. Since her escape from the mental health facility to which her parents' consigned her, Allie has been trying to situate herself in the world.

Because Allie attends so fervently to the present, she must keep a notebook of her memories and plans. In this way, Allie provides a welcome contrast to Barrett, who "had forever cast himself forward from some dark past he could not remember to a future which did not exist" (124). Barrett would prefer to "rest in the quiet center of himself" (124), but he has been unable to. Allie refers to the center of herself as "Sirius," the white dwarf star, "my favorite, diamond bright and diamond hard, indestructible by comets, meteors, people" (93). The need for a center of self that allows one to live in the present moment becomes an essential step for both Allie and Will to function in the world.

A second step towards living in the world is real communication. Until they meet one another, neither Barrett nor Allie communicate authentically with another person. After Allie leaves the hospital, she meets a series of people who all speak to her in clichés or with secondary meanings behind their words. Allie takes "words seriously to mean more or less what they said, but other people seemed to use word as signals in another code they had agreed upon" (34). When a woman attempts to proselytize Allie, the Christian asks questions that are not questions and uses the word "promise" perfunctorily. During Allie's conversation with Richard Rountree, a stranger who pulls up beside her on a park bench, she suspects that he is using words, such as "crash," because "he thought it was the sort of expression she would use" (36). The pretense and dissembling confuses Allie, who prefers to speak to herself through her notebook where she is sure to be understood, or to a dog she adopts, who does not judge her strange but accurate way of speaking.

In *The Second Coming*, the way that people miscommunicate and misuse words becomes of primary concern. While Barrett has grown accustomed to the hypocritical and flimsy way that people speak, after his first exchange with Allie he seems unable to put up with inauthentic dialogue. For instance, Jack Curl attempts to sweet talk Will about his wife, Marion, by saying, "[W]hat a great lady Marion was to give so unendingly of herself. There was so much to give" (126). Cutting through this figurative—and thus ambiguous—language, Barrett responds, "Do you mean because she was so rich or because she was so fat?" (126). Barrett has become disenchanted with feigning talk, so he throws off social norms and asks intentional questions about which he desires answers. As Sutter did to Barrett in *The Last Gentleman*, so Barrett asks Jack Curl, "Do you believe in God?" (*SC* 136). The chaplain struggles to answer adequately the simple, straightforward question. His preference for oblique speech undermines his authority on metaphysical matters. Instead of dialoguing with such obfuscators, Barrett talks to "old mole," or rather to the internalized ghost of his father.

Although Allie and Barrett separate themselves from others out of frustration with inauthentic behavior, they see each other as routes out of isolation. Allie tries without success to decipher "why she felt so free to talk or not talk with" Barrett (109). Both of them speak freely with each other. He interprets easily her odd speech patterns, and she feels safe speaking with him, as though he understands. They feel familiar to one another and exchange words as though trading favors. When Barrett, for instance, explains to Allie that she will need a "creeper" to move the stove, she thanks him for the "gift of the word" (115). Words are things for Allie, and this understanding of language instigates a change in how Barrett communicates as well. He begins to desire her honest way of speaking. Truth, and true speech, provides them the freedom that they seek to act and live in the world.

For Allie, too, Barrett becomes a sign of something more, though she knows not what. After she heals him from his fall, they kiss, and she wonders whether loving him is "the secret, the be-all not end-all but starting point of [her] very life or is it just one of the things creatures do like eating and drinking" (258). Even Allie, for whom words must be things, and who inhabits the world through the present and literal, doubts whether love can be both a sign of something else as well as a physical concrete act. She compares the signs of falling in love to the "signs you recognize when you are getting near the ocean for the first time. Even though you've never seen the ocean before, you recognize it, the sense of an opening out ahead and putting behind the old" (258–59). Loving Barrett is a sign of another love that she has never known and cannot define.

To comprehend "love," Allie seeks first the wisdom of the ages in the library. "Surely great writers and great lovers of the past had written things worth reading," she thinks (240). However, Percy takes a jab at these great writers by listing several clichés on love, to which Allie responds, "These people are crazier than I am" (241). Love is one of the most used-up words in Percy's fiction, yet one that he most hopes to recover. Although Binx in *The Moviegoer* misuses the word "love" with his secretaries, he emphasizes to his brother Lonnie, for whom "words are not worn out," that "it is possible" to say "yes, I love you" (*MG* 162). A word like "love" loses its value through overuse; it becomes meaningless when people equally love ice cream, *The Hulk*, and the Democratic Party. How then do they love God or their neighbor? Just as cheaply? This is why Percy, through the love of Allie and Barrett, attempts to revitalize not only the word but also its meaning.

The battle between love and death is more easily won in Allie than it is in Will. Rather than stay with Allie after falling through her greenhouse, Will returns home. However, instead of Will having only the two alternatives with which the novel began, he now receives three choices: living-death (as a resident of the convalescent home run by his daughter and Jack Curl), suicide with his father's Luger, or the sacramental life with Allie. Barrett attempts to follow his old ways by returning to places of the past, as he did in *The Last Gentleman* when he visited his father's home. He boards a bus to Georgia. Only this time, the memory of Allie compels him to disembark in the middle of the trip. The sun catches a gold poplar "like a yellow-haired girl coming out of a dark forest," and Barrett feels his heart flood with "a sharp sweet urgency, a need to act, to run and catch" (*SC* 297). He feels like he is losing Allie, so he fights the driver to exit the bus, only to end up unconscious—Barrett's third fall.[10]

The novel ends in some way where it began, with medical experts attempting to diagnose what cannot be understood empirically, the behaviors of the soul. Whereas Allie was once under the care of physicians in an insane asylum, now Barrett awakens (he seems to fall unconscious as many times in *The Second Coming* as in *The Last Gentleman*) in a hospital with "great plans being made for him" (*SC* 322). The doctors have diagnosed him with *wahnsinnige Sehnsucht*, or "inappropriate longing" (302). The disorder sounds similar to Tom More's unappeasable desires in *Love in the Ruins*, the desires that led to his return to the Roman Catholic Church. However, in *The Second Coming*, the doctors determine that such longing for transcendent reality is abnormal and must be fixed with an extra hydrogen ion. They consign him to an old folks' home. Although Barrett enjoys his passive existence with his life "out of his hands" (305), thoughts of Allie continually bother him. He wants to see her; he thinks about her, and he wonders, "What was Allie doing?" (310). The two plot lines have begun at opposite places and crossed.

Ultimately, Barrett determines that a life with Allie is the only way to escape the death-in-life plotted out for him by his daughter and practitioners. When Barrett decides to forgo his comfortable existence at the convalescent home, he immediately returns to Allie and steals her away to a Holiday Inn. There the two of them eat from the buffet as though feasting. Throughout the novel, the two have wasted away much of the time without one another. However, together they dine on steaks, corn bread, and apple pie. Unlike his wife's gorging on Little Debbie snacks and stuffing herself with preservatives until she could no longer walk, Allie and Will have an appetite for good food, for each other, and for life. Because of his newfound life in Allie, Barrett throws his two guns into a gorge, which concludes his conversation with his father's ghost and with death itself. Like an ex-suicide, Barrett decides that his father did not miss when he aimed to shoot his son all those years ago. "He killed me then and I did not know it. I even thought he had missed me. I have been living, yes, but it is a living death" (324). This conclusion compels Barrett to choose life with "significance" with Allie, by marrying her—not just legally, but sacramentally—in the Roman Catholic Church (326). Whereas before, both Allie and Will suffered from "inappropriate" or rather, unidentified longings, they now know what they longed for—love, found in each other and perhaps drawn from somewhere else.

The novel does not end with the two of them making love in the Holiday Inn, the trope from the end of *Love in the Ruins,* but with Will returning to the convalescent home to visit with Father Weatherbee in the attic. The priest is substituting for Jack Curl, the heretical chaplain, who is away on a business trip. Although Will declares honestly that he is "not a believer" and has no intention "to enter the church," he does want the priest to perform the marriage sacrament. He also demands that the priest tell him what he knows (358). The final moment echoes the ending of *The Last Gentleman.* As W. L. Godshalk points out, both end with a "comic confrontation with a priest, concerning one of the sacraments, a sacrament that the priest is reluctant to perform."[11] In both *The Last Gentleman* and *The Second Coming* the authority of the priests' message rests outside of themselves—the power of the sacrament rests in Christ. When Jamie questions whether the Gospel is true, Father Boomer answers, "If it were not true, then I would not be here. That is why I am here, to tell you" (*LG* 404). Father Weatherbee asserts similar authority, although in a roundabout way through the story of his mission work in Mindanao. In astonishment the priest explains to Will how the people believed the Gospel: "They said that if I told them, then it must be true or I would not have gone to so much trouble" (*SC* 359).

When Father Boomer made such a declaration, Jamie believed but Barrett missed it. This time, however, Will cries, "Right!" (359) as though he, too, believes the Father's words.

Following his affirmation of Father Weatherbee's impromptu preaching, Barrett asks the question that has plagued him the entire novel: "Do you believe that Christ will come again and that in fact there are certain unmistakable signs of his coming in these very times?" (360). Instead of fearing an apocalypse that must be stopped, such as Tom More dreaded, Will Barrett feels a "secret joy" at the potential answer to this question, an answer the reader never hears (360). However, Father Weatherbee's response is not needed, for Will has discovered the answer himself. He has found the buried treasure and can read the world of signs around him. The last questions are not directed at Weatherbee or the old mole, but are rhetorical questions to which Will knows the answer: "What is it I want from her and him, he wondered, not only want but must have? Is she a gift and therefore a sign of a giver?" (360). As readers have seen over the course of the story, yes, Allie is a sign of a giver. And, yes, Will "will have" both Allie and God, for this is the "third way" that he has been looking for, a way out of death-in-life and away from suicide, a way he may live with meaning and significance (360).

In comparison to Percy's other novels, *The Second Coming* is often lauded as his most resolved work, the only story with a happy ending. Percy himself asserts, "I'm convinced that in *The Second Coming* there's a definite advance, a resolution of the ambiguity with which some of my other novels end: the victory, in Freudian terms, of eros over thanatos, life over death" (*Conversations* 184). It does seem that *The Second Coming* concludes with the loose ends all tied up: Barrett will not commit suicide but will marry Allie and most likely become a Catholic convert. Barrett and Allie will "create a new world," according to Percy (*More Conversations* 74). However, unlike the new order that Lancelot desired to establish with the insane woman next door to his cell, Barrett and Allie will follow Percival's way. In Percy's words, this new world "takes place through the recovery of Christianity" (74).

Yet, critics have noticed that *The Second Coming* is not as clear as Percy liked to think it was. For instance, Godshalk argues that this sequel to *The Last Gentleman* underscores how Barrett's dilemmas are lifelong and unsolvable, and that his "quest for selfhood becomes his misguided quest for God."[12] If Percy aimed at writing an obvious happy ending, there are at least a few readers who debate his success. For Joseph Schwartz, this protagonist is not even Will Barrett but an imposter; he calls the characters from the two novels Will I and Will II to distinguish between them.[13] If Will II is not the same though an older Will I, then the story has failed. Moreover, the connection between the two novels is weak. Percy admits that he did not know his character was Barrett until he was midway through writing the novel, when he then decided to graft "him onto Will's lifeline" (*Correspondence* 260). This grafting complicates depictions of the bold and lusty Kitty Huger with Barrett's former wallflower cheerleader girlfriend. And, the voice of the "last gentleman" has been completely lost, for the elder Will Barrett curses as much as Lancelot does.

Finally, the relationship between Allie and Will is not without signs of problems. The two of them are at least twenty years apart in age, and a couple of times Allie wonders whether Barrett is her biological father (*SC* 109, 260). Whether or not Barrett slept with Kitty is left as an open question (109). Their relationship, in places, sounds similar to Barrett's marriage to Marion. Superficially, both Marion and Allie have grey eyes. More significantly, Barrett married Marion "because he pleased her so much" (156). He enjoyed pleasing Marion as much as Allie enjoys pleasing Barrett. As she says, "It pleases me to please you" (260). In his first marriage, Barrett wanted to marry and "get Jesus Christ in the bargain," but that attempt failed (156). Now he wants to marry Allie and have God as well, but how will this marriage be different? Although it seems that Barrett finally is choosing water over diamonds at the end of *The Second Coming*, he does compare Allie to Sutter: "You're Sutter happy" (263). Her similarities to Kitty and Sutter mark their marriage as potentially problematic.

In addition to its plot problems, the novel itself suffers from some aesthetic gaffes. Linda Whitney Hobson criticizes the book in the first sentence of her essay for "the hero's long interior monologues, which slow down the action."[14] The moments that could have suspense and dramatic action are glazed over, such as Barrett's rescue of Allie from Kitty and Dr. Duk. There is no Wild West showdown that the reader might hope for, not even a verbal sparring like Aunt Emily's denunciation of Binx. Because so much action occurs inside Barrett's mind, it is difficult in places for the reader to follow whether action is real, a memory, or a hallucination. When the action occurs from Allie's perspective, the schizophrenic phrasing and strange language hinder easy reading.

However, the lack of readability and the stylistic abnormalities should not be used to write off Percy's aesthetic merit. Those who accuse Percy of being more of a philosopher or of showing "signs of slippage" in his last two novels are not granting him enough talent as a novelist.[15] His penchant for strangeness in his fiction should be seen in the context of other great novelists, such as Kurt Vonnegut or David Foster Wallace, who do not play by the conventional rules of novel writing. One reviewer, Benjamin De Mott, calls Percy "A Thinking Man's Kurt Vonnegut," a fitting moniker.[16] And Jay Tolson indicates that the hypnotic redundancy and irregular structure of *The Second Coming* owe much to the medium of television and musical composition, respectively.[17] Reviewer Richard Gilman best praises Percy's novel for its overall success despite its perceived flaws:

> I spoke before of Percy's vices being the costs of his virtues. What I came to see as I read his new book was that one had to be willing to grant him his excesses and even his follies. The point isn't that he could somehow learn to give them up, to write more *acceptably*; he writes as he does and can, and if in order to emerge into the clear tonic air of revelation he had to go through much murk and absurdity, so it must be.[18]

Whatever its flaws, the novel enchants readers with its romance, its consideration of big questions, and its attempt at a happy ending. For a world too often attracted to falseness and death, *The Second Coming* offers instead a real love story.

6

The Thanatos Syndrome

Near the end of his life, Walker Percy admitted that, if he were to start all over, he would have liked to have made films (*More Conversations* 136). Percy observed the growing attraction to and increasing familiarity with television and movies in American culture. Wanting to make his ideas accessible to the largest audience, Percy employs cinematic devices in *The Thanatos Syndrome* (1987) to hook readers. Gary Ciuba has likened *The Thanatos Syndrome* to the films *Panic in the Streets* (1950), which tells the story of a public-health employee and a police captain trying to prevent an epidemic of pneumonic plague, and *The China Syndrome* (1979), a thriller about a nuclear power plant's cover up of its dangers to the public.[1] Previously, Percy had written internally focused narratives, but *The Thanatos Syndrome* broke this trend with its quick pace and whodunit plot. Percy's only fear was that the heaviness of the ideas might weigh down the story.

For many critics, Percy's fears were warranted. As a piece of fiction, *The Thanatos Syndrome* was found wanting. *Kirkus Reviews* (March 15, 1987) claims, "Percy [is] bespelled by his own facility at writing lowbrow in a high-brow framework." Critic John Desmond, writing more than a decade after the book's publication, worries that the novel is "too ingeniously plotted and overmanipulated in order to drive home Percy's serious message."[2] However, the work has never seemed to be anything less than what the author intended it to be—a work on par with the fiction of Raymond Chandler, but with longer-lasting value because of the ultimate questions that it asks of readers. For Percy, the "scale of merit" of a novelist was always less important than whether the novelist pursued "the nature of man and the nature of reality" (*MIB* 102). In this case, Percy chose to write a less literary but more broad-reaching suspense novel about a stranger who once again finds himself in a strange land.

As in *The Second Coming,* Percy returns to the story of one of his earlier heroes, this time Tom More from *Love in the Ruins.* When readers last saw More, he was contentedly newly wed to his secretary-nurse Ellen Oglethorpe, the "tyrannical Georgia Presbyterian" (*LIR* 155). Although More has rescinded his madcap delusions of saving the world, he has not overcome his predilection for promiscuous sex and afternoon toddies. Recently, More has been released from prison, after serving two years for selling amphetamines to truck drivers from a way station. His time in prison has taught him to value the small things and forego his grandiose dreams. "Prison does wonders for megalomania," More notes (*TS* 67). He only questions why it took "two years of prison for a man to be able to sit still, listen, notice his children, watch the sunlight on the ceiling?" (*TS* 43). In *Love in the Ruins* More underwent a similar experience after his stay in the insane asylum, where he first learned "to watch and listen" (*LIR* 106). Then, he returned to the world and invented the lapsometer, a portent of his megalomania. Despite More's claims about prison's salvific effects, the reader may doubt whether much has been accomplished.

Although More no longer desires to make a pact "with the Devil to save the world," the church that he embraced at the conclusion of *Love in the Ruins* has become a vague memory; as he admits, "I haven't given religion two thoughts or been to Mass for years" (*TS* 67, 46). Whereas previously the Eucharist saved More from his Luciferean daydreams and transcendental abstraction, now he comforts himself with paying attention to small things, chatting with people, reading books on World War I, and watching sitcom reruns. More has settled into a cozy humanism where he lives a "small life"—much like Binx Bolling, at the start of *The Moviegoer*—and gives God not "a second thought" (*TS* 81). This Tom More appears to be in despair without knowing so.

But More's marriage, family, and local community are in trouble. Although the final line of *Love in the Ruins* pictures Tom and Ellen intertwined in their Sears Best bed, at the beginning of *The Thanatos Syndrome,* they sleep apart in convent beds, which Ellen has purchased according to "high fashion" (50). In *Love in the Ruins*, these beds were a "conceit of Doris's," More's ex-wife (*LIR* 391), beds that he replaces when he marries Ellen. Whether this detail has been misallocated by Percy matters less than what it portends for the Mores' marriage; Ellen is sharing too much in common with More's first wife. Like Doris, who ran away with an Englishman, Ellen now "loves all things English" (*TS* 46). These are small commonalities compared to the fact that Ellen, as Doris did before her, cuckolds her husband. Everyone is embarrassed to speak of More's wife, and there are hints of the affair from Dr. Max Gottlieb, More's colleague, and Hudeen, his housekeeper, but it is not until his cousin Dr. Lucy Lipscomb treats him for Herpes IV that More realizes the betrayal. The doting but directive Ellen from *Love in the Ruins*, who smoothes More's eyebrows with spit from her fingers "like a mother" (*LIR* 155), is replaced by Lucy, who in her "bossy-nurturing, mothering-daughtering way" spits "on her thumb to smooth [his] eyebrows" (*TS* 348). Because his wife, Ellen, too closely resembles his ex-wife, More turns to the arms of a woman who acts more like the woman with whom he fell in love.

If these radical personality transformations were not enough, something else is askew with Ellen. She has taken up competitive bridge, gaining a reputation as a savant. Her partner who is also her lover, John Van Dorn, an international bridge champion, is stunned by her skills. "It is as if she had a little computer stored in her head," he tells More (49). Rather than impress More, this description concerns him. He observes his wife as though she is a patient and notices, "Her eyes do not quite focus on me" (46). Despite their marital problems, the two make love, but not in their usual way. She climbs into bed "on all fours" like an animal, and she performs tricks and utters one-word statements, such as "Azalea" (53). These one-word rejoinders bother More the most. Instead of dialogue, Ellen responds with words from her bridge tournaments. Ellen exhibits "the loss of something" that Tom cannot put his finger on (85).

As in *Love in the Ruins*, More's patients—to whom he adds Ellen—provide evidence "that something strange is occurring" (*TS* 3). "They're somehow—diminished," but More cannot define *how* (85). He notices changes in personality, changes in sexuality, language behavior, context loss, and a strange idiot-savant response. In his tenure as a psychiatrist, More has observed that people pursue two ends in life: either a romantic conception of happiness or the most pleasures possible in life "without getting arrested" (90). He classifies them as bluebirds or jaybirds, respectively. However, whatever syndrome is overtaking his patients is squelching these pursuits. "They've all turned into chickens," More remarks (90). One may recall Flannery O'Connor's quip that this generation is full of "wingless chickens," those for whom "the moral sense has been bred out."[3] In place of anxieties, fears, guilt, or passions, there exists a univocal "sameness" or "flatness" (*TS* 85). In addition to Ellen, More's patients seem both to have digressed and progressed. They're pongid computers, reduced to "pure angelism-bestialism" (180). The loss seems to be a loss of self or loss of their humanity.

What More soon uncovers—through a process of investigation using a high-tech computer, trespassing, two run-ins with both local and federal security officers, and some unsettling firsthand experiences—is a covert operation called the Blue Boy Project, run by John Van Dorn and Dr. Bob Comeaux, in which sodium ions are added to the water supply to placate the population. Blue Boy has reduced crime, child abuse, wife battering, teenage pregnancy, depression, chemical dependence, anxiety, and even AIDS (191). It has succeeded in social engineering. Trying to recruit Tom to join their outfit, Comeaux justifies the experiment with previous cases, as when "we treated dental enamel by fluoride in the water fifty years ago—without the permission or knowledge of the treated" (194). The statistics side with Comeaux's project, but More gets hung up on the moral issue regarding the will of the citizens. After all, this is the same protagonist who wished at the end of *Love in the Ruins* that a man walk into his office "as a ghost or beast or ghost-beast and walk out as a man, which is to say sovereign wanderer, lordly exile" (*LIR* 383). Instead, the Blue Boy Project removes the individual's sovereignty or lordliness and creates ghost-beasts.

The patients that More encounters who are victims of Blue Boy's water additive do show heightened knowledge of trivia and total recall, but they also exhibit disturbing sexual aggressiveness and depleted language skills. The sexual behavior inspired by the ion has motivated Van Dorn's participation in Blue Boy, for he promotes the "sexual liberation of Western civilization" (TS 200). According to Van Dorn, sexual experience is one of the "ultimate goals of being human" (219). Although Van Dorn articulates his "theory of the nature of man" with positive words such as "excellence" and evidence from Mozart and Einstein, readers later discover that Van Dorn is no more than an adulterer, rapist, and pedophile (219).

In *Love in the Ruins* the demonic acts on the surface of the narrative whereas in *The Thanatos Syndrome* its presence is more concealed. Ordinary men, Van Dorn and Comeaux, inherit the wiles of the diabolical Art Immelmann. The battle between angels and demons appears to have yielded to humans at war among themselves. However, this is mere appearance, as revealed by the vision of the Virgin Mary, which Father Smith relates to More. At the end of the novel, Father Smith tells a story of Mary appearing to children in Yugoslavia. She exposes the clever deception of the "Great Prince Satan" who decided the best way to "have his way with men" was to let us be: "No great evil scenes, no demons—[Satan is] too smart for that. All he had to do was leave us alone" (TS 365). According to the vision, when left unto ourselves, we destroy ourselves. Yet Satan's absence is a ploy, for the devil is still having his way.

It is not a coincidence that More moves out of Paradise Estates in *Love in the Ruins* and, having lost Paradise, resides in slave quarters. Percy alludes to *Paradise Lost* in *The Thanatos Syndrome* with the mention of the devil Azazel and by naming Father Smith's assistant Milton. Ellen first mentions "Azazel" in bed with Tom; she uses the bridge term to refer to a sexual act. Unfamiliar with the word, More hears "Azalea" (TS 53). He inquires from Van Dorn the implication of the term and learns it comes from the name of a fallen angel. Van Dorn tells him, "It means you're in a hell of a mess" (61). Azazel was a demon who lived in the Syrian desert, "a particularly barren region where even God's life-giving force was in short supply" (64). The demon becomes a metaphor for the possessed state of Feliciana Parish at the start of the story. According to Hebrew and Canaanite belief, the demon's name was changed once he landed on earth: he became "despair" (64). Just as More misheard the word itself—evidence of his inability to listen to others—so he seems unable to comprehend "despair," especially his own. In Milton's epic, the angel Michael fought against Satan and all his horde, including Azazel. Unfortunately, in *The Thanatos Syndrome*, St. Michael is a "three-foot bronze archangel branding a loose sword, bent at the tip,"[4] and St. Michael's church is an ineffective force against the proliferation of devils.

As a psychiatrist whose medium is the conversation, More is particularly troubled by his patients' inability to articulate thoughts, express emotion, or relate the world to their selves. When More questions Comeaux about the diminished language skills, Comeaux responds, "They're into graphic and binary communication—which after all is a lot more accurate than once upon a time there lived a wicked queen" (197). Comeaux circumvents the problem, but More cuts through his circuitous speech to address the real: "You mean they use two-word sentences" (197). From Comeaux's perspective, this reduction of language ability is not a problem because the benefit of accuracy trumps figurative, imaginative, empathetic story construction. However, for Percy, what separates humans from animals and computers is our ability to participate in triadic behavior, a theory he discusses in detail in his nonfiction works, *The Message in the Bottle* and *Lost in the Cosmos*. Essentially, "triadic" means three parts in relationship with one another. When More visits Father Smith in the watchtower, the priest instructs him on how to situate the coordinates of a fire. Triangulation is needed. The coordinates from Father Smith's tower must be shared with another tower, and their reading helps to locate the blaze. Working in tandem, the two watchers of the respective towers use degrees to communicate the position of the smoke. This action illustrates triadic behavior and provides a metaphor for language. In this example, the degrees signify not only the place of the fire, but also the fire itself. Because of the context of the situation, the two fire-watchers know the meaning of the numbers they exchange and the significance of the numbers. However, language has been deprived of its triadic nature. Words do not always mean what they should, and dyadic communication has replaced triadic conversation. Through More's discoveries, Percy connects the loss of meaning in language with the loss of humanity.

Percy borrows much of his understanding of triadic relations from philosopher C. S. Peirce, which he baptizes with Catholic thought. In *Walker Percy's Search for Community,* John Desmond elucidates the connection between Peirce's semiotic and Percy's theological adoption of it. For both thinkers, the nonmaterial real "exists as an objective reality" with meaning independent of humans' evaluation.[5] Human beings assign words/signs to this objective reality that are both acts "of self-communication" and that "establish an intersubjective relation between persons."[6] Desmond provides a good example: when a lover gives a diamond ring to his beloved, the physical object is a gift itself but also signifies the gift of self from the lover. Within the Catholic Church, this triadic giving occurs in the Eucharist, which is an act of self-communication and the real presence of Christ. For Peirce, "gift giving" is the "quintessential example of triadicity," and Percy applies this account of reality to sacraments.[7] This understanding of the signification of language and of the Eucharist are keystones of *The Thanatos Syndrome,* without which the reader may not be able to read the signs and may lose much of the meaning of the story.

Bob Comeaux exemplifies the problem with obfuscation, for he misuses words to conceal immoral action. Even his name is a lie, which he changed from Como in order to fit in more easily with the southern French-Louisianan locals (*TS* 99). In his case, communication is not self-giving, but rather a game to talk around reality. When Comeaux debates the necessity of eliminating deformed infants, for instance, he prefers the term "pedeuthanasia" instead of "infanticide" because of the latter's "loaded semantics" (36). In the former word, the Greek root *eu* means "good," and thus Comeaux paints the act with positive connotations, whereas the latter has the prefix "-cide" drawn from the Latin *caedere,* which means "to kill." Comeaux employs the word to justify his administration of drugs to end the lives of the unborn, disabled, and aged. Because "*Eu* means good," Comeaux reasons, and "good is better than bad, serenity better than suffering," then what he is doing is morally justified (351). Only at the conclusion of the novel does Comeaux tell the "truth": "I'm the low-class Yankee who does all these bad things like killing innocent babies" (347).

Comeaux provides an example of the loss of signification in words, the primary theme of *The Thanatos Syndrome*. In More's first conversation with Father Smith, the priest explains, "[Words] don't signify anymore" (121). The priest speaks erratically and disconnectedly, and More is distracted by thoughts of Lucy, much as he was with Moira in *Love in the Ruins*. Father Smith's concern that More will "end up killing the Jews" (*TS* 128) is Percy's worry about American doctors who participate in eugenics, euthanasia, and abortion. In Percy's opening note to the novel, he cites Dr. Frederic Wertham's book *A Sign for Cain* as a source for his ideas. Wertham explores the reasoning behind the mass murders at the concentration camps in Nazi Germany, focusing in chapter 9, "The Geranium in the Window" (which will be referred to obliquely by Father Smith), on the deceptiveness of the term "euthanasia": "In reality, these mass killings had nothing whatever to do with euthanasia. [The act] may be called a dysthanasia."[8] Whereas "eu" means "good," the prefix "dys" means "bad" and thus more accurately names the act of mass killing.

In 1981 Percy wrote an article against abortion called "A View of Abortion with Something to Offend Everyone" (*Signposts* 340–42), in which he calls attention to the "doublespeak that the abortionists . . . seem to have hit on in the current rhetorical war" (341). Percy points to language as the initial subterfuge. One can "dispose" of a "fetus" without the guilt one would feel if she or he killed a baby. In *The Thanatos Syndrome*, Percy makes this point indirectly through the dialogues of Comeaux with More over the disposal of "neonates," another word for children under two years old. Comeaux supports his work by citing "*Doe v. Dade*," a thinly veiled indictment of *Roe v. Wade* (*TS* 333). The doctors who manipulate words to cover their egregious acts, or worse, manipulate science to justify their ideology, will inevitably cause more harm than good. Although More has a distaste for Comeaux's work, he understands its logic, which is why Father Smith indicts him.

In Father Smith's confession, he reveals that in his past he, too, succumbed to the logic of people like Comeaux. On a visit to Germany,

Smith sat in on discussions between doctors about the benefits of euthanasia. He recalls reading *The Release of the Destruction of Life Devoid of Value*: "Their arguments made considerable sense to me" (246). During this visit, Smith became enamored with the Hitler Youth Movement and confesses that he would have joined it (248). It is Father Smith's complicity—and More's—that makes them sympathetic accusers. Percy experienced a similar attraction to the Hitler Jugend when he visited Germany in 1934, which is why he could say in a letter to a friend, with much trepidation, "I think we're much more like the Nazis and Dachau than we imagine."[9] For Percy, the humanist logic of American doctors resembled too closely that of the Weimar physicians, and thus, the Holocaust was the next step in the timeline. Father Smith calls Comeaux and Van Dorn "The Louisiana Weimar psychiatrists" (252).

Percy wanted to tackle the horror of the Holocaust because he worried that his own country was quickly becoming a Weimar America. Tolson writes, "Percy's greatest fear was a 'Weimar' America, and to combat such an eventuality he would risk even the integrity of his art."[10] Despite Percy's insistence that he does not give messages in his fiction, he does issue a caution in *The Thanatos Syndrome*: if we are not careful, the Holocaust can happen again. Reviewing William Styron's *Sophie's Choice*, Percy admires his fellow southern writer for the "nerve taking on the Holocaust" (*Correspondence* 258). However, he found the book failed in its attempt. In his opinion, such a task "would take a Dostoevski to do it, and he would by the utmost guile, indirection and circumspection" (258). In addition to Dostoevsky, Percy mentions Vonnegut as the "only novelist" he knows who was able "to get hold of one of our little horrors of the 20th C [sic]" (258). These latter two writers influence Percy's method in *The Thanatos Syndrome*. If Percy is going to tackle the mystery of evil and the subsequent violence of the Holocaust, he must use indirection and circumspection. As he says of Vonnegut, "the only way you can write about such a thing is not to write about it" (*Correspondence* 259). The confession of Father Smith allows Percy the sly angle on the topic.

Percy worried that the sections from Father Smith were too didactic. He tells Shelby Foote, "Every time Fr. Smith opens his mouth he, I, is in trouble" (292). In this letter, Percy conflates Father Smith's words with his own. However, as an author, he realized one "can't get away with a Fr. Zossima [sic] these days and probably shouldn't" (293). He refers to Dostoevsky's saint in *The Brothers Karamazov*, who offers a rebuttal to the atheist Ivan Karamazov and his Grand Inquisitor. In Dostoevsky's novel, the young scientist Karamazov writes a poem entitled "The Legend of the Grand Inquisitor" in which a sixteenth-century Spanish Cardinal rules the people by removing their freedom and appeasing them with food and entertainment, in the form of regular mass bonfires of heretics. To counter this horrific vision, Ivan's younger brother Alyosha records the life of his elder Father Zosima. The priest's hagiography becomes a parable of a life well lived in Christ. In the brief biography, Zosima preaches to and teaches those gathered at his deathbed. While Percy models Dostoevsky in *The Thanatos Syndrome*, he was concerned that such sermonizing would not go over well with his readers. When Percy shared his anxieties with Foote, his friend reaffirmed the "tirades" of Father Smith. Foote writes, "I saw nothing tiradish about it; it never crossed my mind that the confession said anything objectionable whatever—just that it was a very important segment of the novel, maybe even its keystone" (*Correspondence* 294). Indeed, the confession of Father Smith, the preceding dialogue, footnote, and Smith's final sermon are all touchstones of the novel.

As a text within the text, "Father Smith's Confession" is separated from the narrative as an allegory that highlights the meaning behind the plot of the novel. However, even with "Father Smith's Footnote," the protagonist More fails to draw the connection between his own current events and those of Smith's past. More asks a series of questions attempting to understand why Father Smith would tell him such a story; the dialogue saves the episode from becoming too heavy-handed. Moreover, the back-and-forth interview after Smith's story is reminiscent of the Gospel accounts where Jesus would tell a parable and the disciples would beg for an explanation. Father Smith is being as sly as Jesus in his conversation with More. The "sly expression in his eyes"—sly being a modifier More repeatedly uses for Father Smith—signals that he knows more than he communicates explicitly with More.

However, something about the priest's story has aided More in his indecision over the Blue Boy Project. To begin the conversation, More admits to Smith, "I'm not sure what to do" (*TS* 234). Because of the prevalent dishonesty in people's speech, the narrator, More himself, underscores that this assertion is true: "As a matter of fact, I do not know what to do" (234). More finds Comeaux's evidence of social betterment "impressive" and understands "his rationale" (234). Father Smith realizes that he cannot refute Comeaux's argument because "words [have been] deprived of their meaning" (117). The two would be at odds in their use of vocabulary. Percy explains, in his defense of *Love in the Ruins*, "In 1983, you see, we will still be using words like 'freedom,' the 'dignity of the individual,' the 'quality of life' and so on. But the meanings will have slipped" (*Signposts* 248). In other words, Comeaux and Smith would *seem* to agree because both would affirm the dignity of the individual and the quality of life. However, in practice this would mean, for Comeaux, the elimination of deformed children and Alzheimer's patients whereas, for Smith, these phrases mean the protection of human beings' lives no matter their illness or age.

To counteract the obfuscation of language, Father Smith emphasizes honest speech and truth. Instead of directing More or debating with Comeaux, Smith recounts a story from his past. As Flannery O'Connor explained, the purpose of a story is different from an argument: "A story is a way to say something that can't be said any other way.... You tell a story because a statement would be inadequate."[11] In other words, a story embodies a mystery that cannot be reduced to a one-line moral or thesis statement. Father Smith confesses to More, telling the truth about his life, his previous sin, and his guilty conscience. Inverting their roles, Father Smith models for More how to speak truthfully about oneself and provides for him the opportunity to listen attentively to another. He repeats a colloquial phrase, "to tell the truth," to underscore his honesty (*TS* 253). In his confession, Father Smith reveals to More the pervasiveness of dishonesty: "Everyone ... lies" (244). Only when faced with death do people finally tell the truth: "Dying people, suffering people, don't lie. They tell the truth," Father Smith explains. "Death makes honest men of all of us. Everyone is dying too and spending their entire lives lying to themselves. . . . It makes people happy to tell the truth after a lifetime of lying" (244). His confession about his own sins connects with everyone. In his final sermon of the novel, Father Smith repeats this discovery: "Children and dying people do not lie. One need not lie to them. Everyone else lies" (360). Perhaps in this "age of thanatos" (86), when surrounded by death, people will begin speaking truth again. Father Smith's story about his encounter with the Weimar doctors, the Hitler Youth, and eventually the *Kinderhaus* where children were executed at Dachau allows More to experience Smith's protest to Comeaux and Van Dorn's experiment. The story empathizes with More in his complicity in the project, and it reveals the subsequent horror of their logic.

The novel ends when More discovers that at Belle Ame, Van Dorn's progressive school, the teachers are sexually assaulting the students. The cinematic showdown between More and Van Dorn is possibly the funniest episode in the novel, though over-the-top stylistically. As More confronts the Belle Ame staff with photos and videos of their deviant behavior, his Uncle Hugh guards the door of the teachers' lounge with a shotgun. Several try to escape, only to be shot at and minorly wounded on either the rear or the ear. To ensure that the local police will find the group guilty, More forces them all to drink the heavily dosed water that they have imposed on the children. The strong draughts of sodium reduce all of them to chimpanzees, and Percy plays up the farce. Only Van Dorn does not recover quickly from the drugged water, having imbibed too much of it in his past. A stint with a gorilla named Eve in her enclosed habitat eventually recovers his humanity. After exposing the sexual assaults taking place at Belle Ame by Van Dorn and his predatory colleagues, More indicts Comeaux and convinces him to shut down the Qualitarian Centers to avoid arrest. All of the patients are transferred to the hospice at St. Margaret's. Comeaux relocates to the People's Republic of China, where he's been hired as the consultant to the minister for family planning (345). Because China implements social engineering from the top down, Comeaux's transfer to that culture seems fitting. In these neatly tied-up endings, Percy moves from comic to sardonic tone.

This tone changes in the final scenes with Father Smith, who speaks the most significant words in the novel. His final tirade may be Percy's last judgment on his own culture, no matter how much he would deny an explicit connection. When Father Smith does finally preach, he manages "to offend everyone" (357), as Percy himself claims to do in his article on abortion. To hide his personal views and authorial intent, Percy plays up the madness of his speaker and the deafness of the audience. Wearing "rumpled chinos and sneakers," Father Smith stands theatrically before the crowd like a crazy prophet with a cardboard sign "in a New York subway" and announces, "The Great Prince Satan, the Depriver, is here" (358–59). More sits inattentively in the church audience, representing the majority who will be too impaired to hear such a message.

The purpose of *The Thanatos Syndrome* has been to connect humanitarian "tenderness" with the violence of the Holocaust, and Father Smith draws this association in his sermon. Repeating three times what he has stated once before in the novel, Father Smith exclaims, "Tenderness leads to the gaschamber" (360). He then pleads with his audience not to fall for the deception of such philanthropists, but instead to send the "young or old, suffering, dying, afflicted, useless, born or unborn" to the hospice: "Don't kill them! We'll take them—all of them! Please send them to us!" (361). The priest may sound insane to the crowd, but, in his fiction, Percy has always marked such madness as closest to truth. Father Smith acts more like a saint than a madman.

His impassioned calls to action sound similar to speeches made by Mother Teresa. For instance, in her 1985 speech to the United Nations, the saintly woman begged, "Bring us your dying." Earlier Smith contrasts himself with Mother Teresa, but here he models her (244). His former alcoholism casts him in the mold of a whiskey priest like that of Graham Greene's *The Power and the Glory*, a man whose sin did not ultimately overcome his vocation. Moreover, Father Smith has been imitating his patron saint "Simeon the Stylite [who] lived atop a pillar forty feet high and six feet in diameter for twenty years" (*TS* 360). Although Smith appears to be running away from the problems in the world, he is engaging them through the life of an ascetic by praying "for the forgiveness of his sins and the sins of the world below him" (360). Of all of

Percy's priests, only Father Smith resembles the historical saints of the church. And of all the characters in *The Thanatos Syndrome*, only he appears willing to speak truth.

Through his example and emphasis on truth, More has become more honest. When Father Smith requests More to serve Mass routinely at the hospice, he refuses "because honesty is valued above all" (363). Not knowing what to believe and thinking little of religion, More feels it would be deceitful to assist. More underlines the fact, saying, "I told him the truth" (363). More's honesty indicates that he is closer to believing than he realizes. Without intending to, More is "beginning to think like Father Smith" and has started to "listen attentively and with interest" (339). By moving toward honesty and self-forgetting attention, More is approaching the ability to love. Although More has "been deprived of the faith," as Father Smith tells him, the action of belief will supply his faith (364).

Percy does not clarify how More's faith will be returned to him, but the clues have been implicit in the narrative. By assisting the Mass, More is engaging in triadic behavior. Although Father Smith refuses to preach, he still conducts Mass because the actions signify. To illustrate his point, Father Smith asks More to define "sacrament." Rattling off his catechism, More responds, "A sensible sign instituted by Christ to produce grace" (125). While the words may mean little in this time and place, the "sign" of the sacrament, such as the Eucharist, retains its signification. Christ's bodily presence has not evacuated the appearance of bread and wine. Therefore More is giving not only himself but also the body and blood of Christ to the parishioners. Because the Eucharist still signifies, More participates in the mysterious triadic relationship between what Percy calls the real, sign, and interpretant. To highlight the significance of More's engagement in giving, Percy concludes with More's agreement to assist at Mass on Epiphany. In the Roman Catholic calendar, the Epiphany liturgy celebrates the baby Christ's reception of the three Magi, who express their faith by giving to Christ frankincense, gold, and myrrh. Not only does the feast day recall the gift-giving but also the revelation of the Incarnation to those beyond the Jews. These pilgrims from afar received light in their darkness, as the Roman Catholic Church reminds its members, and the laudable response is to give.

Percy contrasts More's inkling of faith with his wife's fervor for Pentecostalism to show that, despite his lack of zeal, More at least lives in a world of signification. Ellen "loves the Holy Spirit, [but] says little about Jesus" and cannot decipher the signs of the liturgical Epiphany (353). When Father Smith calls to ask More to assist at Mass, he uses a "code" to avoid her detection (270). Ellen disapproves of the "Catholic trafficking in bread wine, oil, salt, water, body, blood, spit—things," and so she dislikes More's involvement in the church (353). To prevent upsetting her, the priest only hints of the nature of his call: "Royalty, a visit, gifts and—a Jewish connection" (369). Ellen is unable to read the signs; she thinks a noble Sephardic family from Spain may be requiring More's psychiatric services. In contrast to Ellen, for More, things signify. His faculty for decoding the priest's message indicates a potential return to signification and the world of the real.

The final episode occurs in the same place where the novel began, but the repetition emphasizes that More has improved. A common structure in Christian narrative is the spiral view of time, not as a line as the Jews view it or a cycle as the Greeks saw it, but as a combination of the two.[12] Time cycles while ascending, so that events build ever upward. In the opening scene, More visits one of his patients, Mickey LaFaye, in the hospital. "Well well well," she says, "My old pal Doc" (7). Although More has not seen her since he was in prison, he notes, "*Never*, not in a state of terror or out of it, would she have called me that" (7). Mickey's impropriety instigates More's search for the source of her and everyone else's strange behavior. Now, after More has uncovered the social-engineering experiment and Mickey has been detoxed of the heavy sodium doses, she returns to see him as a patient. She begins telling him of a dream in which a stranger is trying to communicate. "I think the stranger is part of myself," she asserts. "I am trying to tell myself something" (371). Repeatedly, we have seen this situation in Percy's fiction: someone wants to tell someone something but cannot rightly communicate. At the conclusion of *Lancelot*, for example, the monologist stops ranting and asks, "Do you have something to tell me?" (*L* 252) and in *The Second Coming*, Barrett asks Weatherbee, "[Do] you have something to tell me, do you?" (*SC* 358). We do not hear Mickey's news from her stranger, for after she "opens her mouth to speak," the final words of the novel are "Well well well" (*TS* 375). This closing line is not in quotation marks, so it is unattributed to either character. We have heard Mickey utter these words before, but with flatness and from her drugged-up state. At the end of the novel, how are these words to be interpreted?

In some ways, we have returned to the beginning, but there has been a development. Mickey's "Well well well" does not represent the empty syllables of the possessed but the hopeful affirmation of both the doctor and his patient. It is good news, though in coded form. The repetition of "well" recalls St. Julian of Norwich's conclusion, "All shall be well, and all shall be well, and all manner of things shall be well."[13] This is not the first age of *thanatos*, nor shall it be the last. The gas chambers existed, and social engineering continues in various guises. Yet, the mysterious utterance of St. Julian is somehow true. With this ending, Percy reminds us that, although there will be fires, the saints will be watching from their towers.

APPENDIX
Lost in the Cosmos

Through a strange instance of serendipity, I was introduced to Walker Percy's cult classic, *Lost in the Cosmos: The Last Self-Help Book*. After spending a month holed up in a windowless room reading Percy's novel manuscripts in the University of North Carolina–Chapel Hill's library, I was boarding a plane to return home. Next to the plane door, leaning up against the side of it, as if on display, was a first edition of *Lost in the Cosmos*, a library copy covered in plastic with a stamp on its side. Percy had left the confines of study and entered my world. The book was begging to be picked up, but every other traveler had passed by without seeing it. I felt drawn to this abandoned book as though someone had left it for me. I picked it up. As I read it on the flight, I laughed aloud the whole way home. Ever since my first reading, I cannot stop recommending the book as an introduction to Percy's work. So many people have stories about how this book changed their lives. The book demands response. Love it or loathe it, *Lost in the Cosmos* acts as a litmus test of the human self.

Published in 1983 as a response to Carl Sagan's *Cosmos* (1980), *Lost in the Cosmos* was Percy's most popular work, selling more than any of his other titles. Sagan's book accompanied his widely popular PBS series by the same title, a show that reached more viewers globally than any in PBS history. Both the book and the show propagate the scientism that Percy spent his life combating. Although once a believer in scientism himself, Percy knew that, as much as science could tell us about the world around us, when it came to the self, the human being, *homo sapiens*—or what Percy calls *homo loquens* or *homo symbolificus*—science need be silent.[1] Yet it wasn't. Carl Sagan, with his full faith in the all-extensive reach of science—claimed to know what cannot be known. And 500 million people believed him.

Appendix: *Lost in the Cosmos*

As always, Percy was concerned with how to reach his audience. He would not be able to host a competing TV series. Not to mention, one of the things Percy was trying to get at was the negative effects of extensive TV watching (this from a man who devotedly watched daytime soaps and *The Incredible Hulk*).[2] If Percy wanted to reach masses of people with a message to counter Sagan's, he needed a book that was fun to read. *Lost in the Cosmos* is zany, scandalous, sarcastic, and funny. Thankfully, Percy revoked his preliminary titles, "Son of Message in the Bottle" and "Novum Organum," choosing instead the more accessible and timely *Lost in the Cosmos*. His previous book on the same topic, *The Message in the Bottle*, lacks the comedic tone, is more direct, drier, and has no diagrams. *The Message in the Bottle* is a collection of essays, two of which were meant to act as bookends, written in the year of publication (1975), tying Percy's thoughts together. However, it is difficult to slough through essay after essay on the same thesis. The vocabulary and density of the ideas is more off-putting than inviting. As one reviewer writes twenty years later, "*The Message in the Bottle* is to *Lost in the Cosmos* as It's a Small World is to Mr. Toad's Wild Ride."[3] Because of its wildness, the book quickly gained popularity.

One of the first things that readers must realize about *Lost in the Cosmos* is that it's funny. The satirical parody has been lost on many a bookseller who stored the book on the shelf suggested by its subtitle, "The Last Self-Help Book." Most self-help books do not begin with such a sobering and riddling epigraph: "We are unknown, we knowers, to ourselves. . . ." Nietzsche's quote is an admonition to know ourselves while also facing the truth that we are unable to do so. The self-help that Percy will ultimately offer is that we are unable to help ourselves. Such a thesis hardly sounds funny. It should not be surprising, then, that many people miss the joke. Whatever humor is to be found is weighted heavily by truth.

Percy worried the book was too "smart-ass and maybe even mean," not to mention vulgar with its foul language and racy content.[4] He was concerned that he had gone overboard in places, was more insulting than satirical. "The trick of the satirist," Percy tells a friend, "is to use

Appendix: *Lost in the Cosmos*

the rapier not the sledge, and slip it in without the reader even knowing. And above all to stay light-footed."[5] If Percy hammered too hard, the point would be lost, as it was and is for some readers. They find the apologetic too preachy or the project itself implausible. I've heard readers want to stop after the first few pages because they felt that Percy was making fun of them. While the book is addressed to "you," keep in mind Percy's intention. The book is not an attack by a bully, but more of a "choose your own adventure" to find out what's wrong with the world and to get under your skin to help you find out, what's wrong with you? Whether we get the joke becomes a gamble over whether we will know or understand our very self, which is why Percy's book is both funny and serious.[6]

Instead of a chapter-by-chapter approach, Percy divides the book into five parts: a preliminary short quiz, a twenty-question multiple-choice self-help quiz, a semiotic primer of the self, and a two-part space odyssey that all address the problem of the self that Percy proposes: how can we know so much about everything else in our cosmos and so little about ourselves? Before you even discover the book's structure, Percy presents a page of alternate subtitles, which should key someone into the comic tone, but which also provides hints at the thesis of the work. Each subtitle is approximately three lines. One should deduce that this book is not your average "10 Ways to Get Thin Quick" or "How to Satisfy Your Man in a Parking Lot" type book. The list of subtitles includes gratuitous hyperbole, false statistics, and an emphasis on the repeated word "strange." One subtitle reads, "The Strange Case of the Self, Your Self, the Ghost which Haunts the Cosmos." If this were the title of a mystery novel, it implies that you, Reader, are the villain, the mystery, and the victim, all in one. Percy switches gears in the next four subtitles, using questions to inquire about this problem of the self. The mystery becomes not only addressed to the reader but also located outside the pages of the text. Percy demands that this book not be one to close and forget. It does not target a small demographic; it is meant to be read by everyone, everywhere. And, in spite of its timeliness, it may be Percy's most timeless text.[7]

Appendix: *Lost in the Cosmos*

TRIADIC VERSUS DYADIC COMMUNICATION

In *The Message in the Bottle,* Percy tried to establish a theory of humanity based on humans' unique capability to speak to one another. He claims, "Since no other creature but man uses language, it is really an anthropology, a study of man doing the uniquely human thing" (11). The premise that no other creature uses language may be questionable.[8] However, Percy argues that human language is divergent from other creatures' because of our use of symbols. He contrasts human language with B. F. Skinner's research with pigeons, who were taught to peck certain buttons to obtain food, or Sue Savage-Rumbaugh's gorillas, who learned American Sign Language. The direction of communication for these animals is one to one—dyadic. Whereas animals participate in dyadic communication, humans use language metaphorically and symbolically. For instance, we hear "My love is like a red, red rose," or we say, "She's a brick house," and we understand the literal as well as figurative meanings. We recognize signification in the signs. Moreover, the relationship between signs and signified also involves a sign giver and receiver. Because the relationship is triadic, it is necessarily social.[9] For Percy, this difference between dyadic and triadic marks humans as qualitatively set-apart beings.

The triadic nature of language marks Percy's first step in confronting Cartesian dualism. René Descartes begins his project by locating the self in the mind, and it is this capacity to think that grants him existence. This famous assertion, "I think therefore I am" is responsible for the "Cartesian split," the divide of the self into body and mind, and the subsequent division of the world into concrete, empirical reality versus abstract ideas. Percy blames the French Enlightenment thinker for the beginning of the confusion:

> The Self since the time of Descartes has been stranded, split off from everything else in the Cosmos, a mind which professes to understand bodies and galaxies but is by the very act of understanding marooned in the Cosmos, with which it has no connec-

tion. It therefore needs to exercise every option in order to reassure itself that it is not a ghost but is rather a self among other selves.

Although Percy drafts this claim as one answer among many for his question about promiscuity, it resonates with what he writes in other essays and in his fiction. In contrast to Descartes, Percy defines the self as "among other selves." The essential socialness of human beings (as opposed to Descartes's "I") becomes one of the main correctives of Percy's endeavor in *Lost in the Cosmos*.

The "I" in Descartes's system becomes relegated to the "We." Percy finds it impossible to know anything apart from other people. Even the word "consciousness" shows a connection to other people, for etymologically, it means, "I know with" (*LIC* 105). "What Descartes did not know: no such isolated individual as he described can be conscious" (105). According to Percy's theory of language, consciousness relies on interaction. The world of the sign user relies upon other sign givers and receivers. Percy addresses this conclusion to the reader: "You are also a co-namer, co-discoverer, co-sustainer of my world—whether you are Kafka whom I read or Betty who reads this. Without you—Franz, Betty—I would have no world" (101). While creatures who communicate through dyadic modes reside in an environment, Percy emphasizes that the triadic creature acts within a world, one which relies on other triadic creatures.

With this premise, Percy begins *Lost in the Cosmos* as a dialogue with the reader. The opening sentence invites triadic communication: "Imagine that you are reading a book about the Cosmos." Rare is the book whose first line tells you to imagine reading a different book. It throws you off. You thought you could lie in bed with the lamp on or the Kindle glowing and passively consume Percy's text, but you can't. He won't let you. Instead, Percy begins playing a game, which continues throughout the rest of the book. This opening section offers a series of five thought experiments, written mostly as questions, concluding with a list of different types of selves to choose from. As in his fiction, Percy's agenda here is that, at some point, for at least one question, you think, "Yes, I do that. Yes, I'm like that. Yes, this has happened to me." If so, then he has you hooked, and you keep reading.

THE PROBLEM OF THE SELF

Percy explicitly recognizes a problem in reaching his audience with this message: how to bring another self into dialogue about its self when it does not know what it is? In Percy's triadic world of signs, how do we locate the self? What is the sign for the self? In previous ages, religious meta-narratives defined the self, and people could believe in versions of signification that explained how their selves fit in the world. The problem of dislocation, then, is modern. Percy phrases it this way: "In a post-religious technological society, these traditional resources of the self are no longer available: self conceived as immanent, consumer of the techniques, goods, and services of society; or as transcendent, a member of the transcending community of science and art" (113). An unnatural dichotomy has been drawn between transcendent and immanent—the Cartesian split—and people who use either method of identification feel dissatisfied with their options.

The "Twenty Question Quiz" near the start of the book seems like a collective mess, but the headings all reference a particular type of "self" that Percy has observed: amnesiac, bored, fearful, envious, promiscuous, to name a few. These modifiers diagnose maladies that Percy considers universal (or, at least, Western). While they read like medical conditions or psychological disorders, the titles poke fun at the current penchant among scientific experts to classify the problems of the self. Percy's questions are tricky. Not only is there no right answer, but each question makes you evaluate your life and pay attention to things you've probably never examined before. Socrates said, "The unexamined life is not worth living." Like Socrates, Percy interrogates the reader toward truth. The conundrum reminds me of a "Far Side" cartoon in which cows are feeding in a field when one of them looks up and exclaims, "Hey wait a minute! This is grass! We've been eating grass!" Percy's questions to the reader induce this kind of revelation. They make you

Appendix: *Lost in the Cosmos*

stop and scratch your head and say, "Wait a minute. . . ." The "Thought Experiments" that follow perpetuate this defamiliarization with their variety of genres—parables, journals, and even a screenplay for "The Last Donahue Show." These questions should incite you to reconsider the ways you have previously constructed your identity and ask, *how do I know myself?*

On the one hand, Percy describes the consumer, immanent self, which longs for something more than buying groceries, attending PTA meetings, and balancing the checkbook. These selves have relegated all of their problems to the realm of the scientists and artists who offer them moments of transcendence in "scientific" discoveries about the self (think of the fun of WebMD or Internet quizzes that identify your personality type) or in the pages of a novel when a character reflects your own face as in a mirror. The cult of the experts feeds off these consumers. Percy saw the popularization of pseudoscience gaining momentum in his decade: "[N]owadays there is no piece of nonsense that will not be believed by some and no guru or radio preacher, however corrupt, who will not attract a following" (172). The consumer is desperate for a solution to his or her boredom, loneliness, depression, impotence, obesity, alienation, and so on. Yet, every time consumers buy into the propaganda of the experts, they are disappointed with the purchase.

On the other hand, the transcendent self of the artist or scientist cannot escape enough from the physical world to satisfy the longing for transcendence. The latest scientific finding offers a momentary high. The successful sonnet grants a brief vision of the heavens before the poet once again must clip his toenails. And, "there's the rub," Percy points out. "[T]he spectacular miseries of reentry. . . . It is difficult for gods to walk the earth without taking the form of beasts" (124). One glimpses heaven for but a minute and must return again to earth. Moreover, the relationship to other people becomes patronizing or condescending. When you are transcendent, everyone else becomes lower. If not, then you have warring gods in the air fighting for turf. As Percy notes, "Two gods in the Cosmos is one too many" (124). Such interaction is unsustainable, for no one can ride a high horse into eternity. And, it has too often been proven that the great geniuses of the world needed somebody to love. However, you can't hold someone's hand if you're floating ten feet above them.

Neither the possibilities of the immanent or the transcendent self are enriching because both are incomplete forms of self-identification. They suffer from the Cartesian divide in which the options are: be a physical organism or be a floating head; be a sexual beast or be an angelic thinker. How to be both? How to be a creative animal or a spirit with hands and feet? Moreover, the assumption popularized by scientism and media is that each self is autonomous, a god who makes his/her own world. If one is a physical god, then the erotic takes possession. However, if one is a transcendent god, then the demoniac or violent spirit is in charge. As Percy mentioned earlier, the autonomous and divided self will prove itself to itself through sex or war.[10]

THE FALLACY OF THE AUTONOMOUS SELF

In the middle of the book is a "Semiotic Primer of the Self," which Percy slyly suggests one can skip. However, this "intermezzo" is really the "keystone" section.[11] In it Percy confronts the destructive belief in the autonomous self. First, Percy claims that language defines human beings. Second, he illustrates the unavoidable social aspect of this phenomenon, in effect proving that human beings are by nature social creatures. He even goes so far as to suggest consciousness is never isolated. Why does he feel it is so necessary to prove the social root of language? Because of the prevalent belief in self autonomy and its calamitous consequences. Percy blames the horrors of the twentieth century on this fallacy: "the autonomous self who, believing in nothing, can fall prey to ideology and kill millions of people—unwanted people, old people, sick people, useless people, unborn people, enemies of the state—and do so reasonably, without passion, even decently, certainly without the least obnoxiousness" (*LIC* 157). In *The Thanatos Syndrome* Percy will repeat this list through the voice of Father Smith. The autonomous self leads to euthanasia, abortion, and genocide, all without regret and even with rational justification.

Without an outside authority—like the God of Islam, Judaism, or

Appendix: *Lost in the Cosmos*

Christianity—the self must determine its own purposes, reasons for existence, and best course of actions. "By and large, scientists and artists and the autonomous self have gotten rid of God," Percy observes (*LIC* 157). Recall that scientists and artists are the transcendent selves who rival god with their "transcendence." The by-product of a science that rules out a creator, or because of its success in healing and advancing technologically no longer needs the aid of an omnipotent being, is an autonomous self.

Left in charge of itself, Percy claims, "the autonomous self in a modern technological society is possessed. It is possessed by the spirit of the erotic and the secret love of violence" (178). Percy borrows these ideas from Kierkegaard, but applies them to a twentieth century in which all other modes of being have been found wanting.[12] Work has become dull and repetitive. Marriage and family life do not fulfill our "Brady Bunch" idealized versions. High-school physics and English classes have managed to even make Newton's laws and Shakespeare's plays boring. Politics are shallow, churches are dispirited, and Mardi Gras only lasts a week. What's left for self-enjoyment, or distraction from the banality of existence, but travel, sports, media, drugs, and sex? Percy lists these last five and then crosses each one off the list except for sex, the cheapest and most available of the five. The driving force of a life free from the constraints of old metaphysics and legalistic superstitions is sex.

Percy ties together the erotic and violent spirits of the autonomous self, seeing them as two sides of the same coin. Inquiring, "The spirit of violence in the coming technological sexually liberated age?" Percy answers, "Here is the great problematic" (191). Without the dialectic with Christianity, sexual behavior holds no bounds. Will such a new world launch a revolution in freedom and a more peaceful society, or will this trivialization of the erotic bring about World War III? The latter seems more probable to Percy, hence his apocalyptic depictions in *Love in the Ruins* and *Lancelot*. In the final sections of *Lost in the Cosmos*, Percy examines the world after this apocalypse has occurred.

Despite such seeming pessimism regarding the autonomous self, Percy leaves room for the small chance that a few faithful followers of Christ may survive the fallout. The only way to survive is "under the direct sponsorship of God" (156). Percy quotes Kierkegaard from *The Sickness Unto Death*: "[T]he self can only become itself it if does so transparently before God" (156). He lists those who have "become themselves transparently before God and managed to live intact through difficult lives": Simone Weil, Martin Buber, Dietrich Bonhoeffer, and Flannery O'Connor. In these examples, we see those who have submitted their autonomous freedom to the direction of a divine power, God.

Percy charts a semiotic profile of such a survivor in an absurd scene that occurs at the Taos Indian Pueblo. A young Indian dancer reenacts a sacred corn dance with an old Indian dancer—one for the money and the second because of his beliefs. In this scene, several characters gather to observe the dance, each of whom represents a different level of transcendence or immanence. Among the tourists is a Catholic priest, the only one who exemplifies a self that knows itself. Although imperfect—with an apathetic stance towards his duties and a temptation to Bushmills—the priest is a "humble and mediocre man," who "is a pilgrim and wayfarer not at home in this world and bound for his true home elsewhere" (139). For Percy, the wayfarer describes all human beings, and this priest's recognition of himself as such is evidence that survival is possible *before* the world ends.

PROPHECY AGAINST DESTRUCTION

The final two sections of the book are entitled "Space Odysseys" and are prophecies of what the future may look like should we "lost" human beings continue charting the course that we are on. Like all of Percy's prophecies, he writes them in the hopes that we may be dissuaded from such a future. However, in case we instead manage to destroy our world, Percy also provides two possible paths for living in the ruins.

Most of the first odyssey occurs in a dialogue between a second officer of a lost earthship and an extraterrestrial intelligence on Proxima Centauri's third planet (PC3). The earthship is held in orbit until the extraterrestrials can determine whether their species will be destructive or able to flourish on their planet. They must answer a series of questions to determine what kind of beings they are. The PC3's questions reveal that the earthship is full of "hostile," "deceptive," and "cruel" creatures. Because of their unseemly desire to "screw" any creatures on PC3, the earthlings (C2s) are not permitted to land. Despite this evidence of C2's destructive nature, the earthship commander adamantly insists that they do not need help: "We help ourselves. We are the triumphant emerging species on our planet, and though we are not as far advanced as you, we are not ashamed of our scientific and technological and artistic achievements. If we were not a tough, self-sufficient, inquisitive species, we wouldn't be here" (215).

By engaging in these questions and viewing one's self from an outside—even alien—perspective, the reader may realize the need for help from beyond the self. More than that, readers might begin to recognize their flawed understanding of the self and seek for a new anthropology that makes one not an autonomous Cartesian self nor a consuming organism but a symbol-using communal creature whose nature is both transcendent and immanent.

Percy credits Walter Miller's *A Canticle for Leibowitz* for much of the adventure that he writes in this second odyssey. Percy reviewed Miller's novel in 1971 and found it "high-class sci-fi pulp" but with a "secret," a message that cannot be told because the telling "ruins it" (*Signposts* 227). You either get it or you don't, Percy argues. The same may be true of Percy's second space odyssey. A space crew sets out on an investigatory journey to find extraterrestrial help for a failing earth. After nearly five hundred years for earth but only eighteen years for the crew, the ship lands in Utah to find a mere handful of survivors on earth. Nuclear disaster has ravaged the planet and the human population, so the survivors must debate how to carry on post-apocalypse. Percy details two proposals: whichever option the reader considers the most appealing will reveal much about his/her self. On the one hand is an Enlightenment dystopia called New Ionia. This society will be sexually liberated, unencumbered by religion, and full of arts and science. After reading the other 90 percent of *Lost in the Cosmos*, the reader should be wary of this projected utopia. The alternative to New Ionia is a democratic settlement primarily populated by holy fools, disabled children, and a few atheist humanists who enjoy the ordinary pleasures of the good life. A reader of Percy will not miss the author's bias toward the latter alternative.

THE LAST SELF-HELP BOOK

As often happens with Percy's ambiguity and indirection, readers miss his implicit message in *Lost in the Cosmos*. In his initial review in the *New York Times*, Anatole Broyard found the book unconvincing and pessimistic with regard to the potential of the self.[13] Even several decades after its original publication, reviewers focus on the negative and not the implied positive. One writer finishes Percy's book with a joyous rallying for our "hollow selves" to "travel on" in spite of having "no real direction home."[14] Now those comments might have Percy somersault in his grave. For these readers, the book leaves nothing but empty roads and broken gods. But Percy saw tearing down the jungle as only step one; in step two, he was trying to water the Sahara. Where readers saw only a diagnosis of homelessness and alienation, Percy hoped to imply an unearthly home and a transcendent community.

Being the great diagnostician that he was, Percy had spent that time paying attention to the oddities of his culture, what he calls the "anomalies of modern times," like the rise of boredom and suicide in a country that has the pursuit of happiness in its founding documents. He felt that all the disparate observations—TV junkies, pigeons and chimps learning to talk, the fascination with horrific news headlines—all of these antinomies were connected, but no one wanted to say how. Leaving no sacred cow untipped, Percy runs through the American pasture flipping over our idols until all we can see is the object worthy of our worship. If *Lost in the Cosmos* succeeds, it will be the "last self-help book" because the self will realize it needs not merely helping but saving, and this salvation cannot come from the self.

NOTES

INTRODUCTION

1. Qtd. by Rod Dreher, "Walker Percy Bourbon Tour."
2. In his collection of autobiographical essays, Christian Wiman describes the state of this generation as "Being From Nowhere": "We often simply won't ask each other where we're from, skirting the question as if it is too intimate, or, more likely, too involved to broach" (*Ambition and Survival* 6).
3. Samway, *Walker Percy: A Life* 3.
4. Other scholars have chased the influence of Percy's ancestry, notably Bertram Wyatt-Brown in *The House of Percy* or Edward J. Dupuy in *Autobiography in Walker Percy*.
5. *Thanatos Syndrome* viii. Also, in a defense of Louisiana, Percy writes, "I chose Louisiana, thirty-eight years ago, and do not intend to live anywhere else" (*Signposts* 67).
6. William Alexander Percy writes, "Was he a pirate? Or the lost heir of the earls of Northumberland? Or a hero of the Spanish wars? Silence. Mystery" (*Lanterns* 39).
7. William Percy, *Lanterns* 39.
8. See Wyatt-Brown's *The House of Percy*.
9. Cash, *Mind of the South* 3.
10. William Percy, *Lanterns* 40.
11. In a letter to Shelby Foote (March 4, 1978), Walker Percy reflects on his upcoming sixty-fifth birthday: "I've lived longer than any Percy in history and therefore have no precedent. [. . .] What's interesting is the apocalyptic feeling: that anyday I'll get tapped on the shoulder by the family ghost: OK, it's your turn now, pull the sugar kettle over your head and jump in the Bogue" (*Correspondence* 239).
12. In response to his legacy of suicide, his father's death in particular, Walker insisted, "I was determined not only to find out why [my father killed himself] but also to make damn sure that it didn't happen to me" (*Pilgrim in the Ruins* 73).
13. Wyatt-Brown uses this image at the start of *The House of Percy* as a metaphor for the Percy line (3).
14. In Søren Kierkegaard's *Fear and Trembling*—an influential text on Percy—the author compares the "knight of infinite resignation" to that of faith (67). The former, with whom Will Percy would identify, resigns himself to defeat, whereas the latter continues in duty to God despite the appearance of defeat.
15. William Percy, *Lanterns* 312.

16. In *Love in the Ruins,* the nutty Mr. Ives wants to return to his farm, "Lost Cove," to "[w]rite a book, look at the hills, live till I die" (234). In *The Second Coming,* Lost Cove is the name of the cave where Barrett goes to commit suicide. In *Lost in the Cosmos,* Lost Cove is the fallout community where Captain Schuyler and Jane go to restart human civilization.

17. Qtd. by Wyatt-Brown, *The House of Percy* 303.
18. Coles, *An American Search* 66.
19. Percy, *Signposts* 271.
20. Percy, "Physician as Novelist," *Signposts* 192.
21. Tolson, *Pilgrim in the Ruins* 191.
22. Ibid., 126.
23. Percy, *Signposts* 304.
24. O'Connor, *Habit of Being* 131.
25. Excerpt undated, sent attached to a letter from Gordon to Andrew Lytle dated April 4, 1952 (Gordon Papers, Princeton University Library).
26. At eleven years old, LeRoy accidentally shot himself in the stomach with a shotgun, which had been a recent present from his father.
27. William Percy, *Lanterns* 95.

CHAPTER ONE

1. Auden, "The Unknown Citizen," lines 1–2.
2. Martin Heidegger was a twentieth-century German philosopher, one of the handful of existentialists whom Percy read. In *The Heidegger Dictionary,* Daniel O. Dahlstrom defines "Everydayness" as "the way of being that is nearest to us, yet repeatedly skipped over" (69).
3. Kierkegaard, *The Sickness Unto Death* 110.
4. Solzhenitsyn, "A World Split Apart," June 8, 1978.
5. The reference to "Banquo's ghost" is from Shakespeare's *Macbeth.* After Macbeth has murdered the king, the slain soldier, a loyal subject of the previous king, returns to haunt Macbeth at a formal dinner, but only Macbeth can see him.
6. The number was compiled by Woods Nash in "*The Moviegoer*'s Cartesian Theater," 36.
7. In the original but unpublished manuscript of *The Moviegoer,* Binx's father had more significance. Binx's search was primarily a search for his father. Instead, Percy marginalizes this influence in the published version but emphasizes that Binx has inherited a romantic conception of the world.
8. Kierkegaard—a nineteenth-century Danish philosopher thought to be the originator of "existentialism"—is a major influence on Percy's writing. In contrast to other existentialists, however, he was a Christian and focused on theological problems.
9. Charles Taylor defines "secular age" as one in which faith is a choice among many

alternative life options; it has become the defining feature of the Western world (*A Secular Age* 3).

10. It is also a current radio spot on National Public Radio (thisibelieve.org/about/).
11. Amato, "Walker Percy's Critique," 49.
12. Lewis, *The Weight of Glory* 1.
13. Lewis, *Surprised by Joy* 41.
14. Percy quotes the same passage on his essay on "Stoicism in the South" (*Signposts* 84).
15. John Carr interview, *Conversations* 66.
16. Aunt Emily is an obvious reincarnation of Will Percy. Despite her shortcomings, it is not an unflattering portrayal. Walker admired his uncle as much as Binx admires his aunt, so much so that Walker dedicates this book to him.
17. Walker writes this apology of his uncle's classicism and racism in his introduction to *Lanterns on the Levee*: "[I]t is hardly proper to judge a man's views of the issues of his day by the ideological fashions of another age" (xii). He gives examples of the problem with looking backwards in judgment, noting that Lincoln was a segregationist while Will Percy was regarded in his day as a "flaming liberal and nigger-lover" (xiii).
18. Rory Calhoun was a 1950s actor who starred in several Westerns and a few blockbuster films with leading ladies such as Marilyn Monroe and Betty Grable. Known more for his sexual liaisons with his costars or female reporters, Calhoun is a fitting dialogue partner for this scene.
19. Letter from Stanley Kauffmann to Walker Percy, February 5, 1960, folder 14, Walker Percy Papers #4294.
20. Letter from Stanley Kauffmann to Elizabeth Otis, Percy's agent, October 21, 1959, Walker Percy Papers #4294.
21. Kierkegaard, *The Sickness Unto Death* 69.

CHAPTER TWO

1. Coles, "The Doubtful Pilgrim," *New York Times*, June 8, 1997.
2. Desmond, *Walker Percy's Search for Community* 83
3. In a 1966 review in LIFE magazine, Walter Goodman asks rhetorically, "Didn't we meet Williston, under another name, as *The Moviegoer* . . . ?" (20).
4. In a letter to Caroline Gordon regarding his choice to start with a young man thinking in Central Park, Percy writes, "[W]hat with the times being what they are, one almost has to begin a book with a solitary young man. All my writings, for better or worse, take off from this solipsism which Allen described in his essay about Ode to the Confederate Dead. The best I can do is break him out of the solipsism" (undated, Tuesday, box 35, folder 24, Caroline Gordon Papers).
5. Tate, *Essays of Four Decades* 595
6. Ibid., 594

7. Both have similar résumés. The Misfit says, "I been almost everything. Been in the arm service, both land and sea, at home and abroad, been twice married, been an undertaker, been with the railroads, plowed Mother Earth, been in a tornado, seen a man burnt alive once . . ." (*Collected Works* 149). Likewise, Mr. Shiftlet "had been a gospel singer, a foreman on the rail road, an assistant in an undertaking parlor, and he had come over the radio for three months with Uncle Roy and his Red Creek Wranglers. He said he had fought and bled in the Arm Service of his country" (175). I made this observation first in a 2008 article, "Individualism in Flannery O'Connor's *A Good Man Is Hard to Find*" (198).

8. By using scientific vocabulary such as "noxious particles," to describe how Barrett sees the world, Percy satirizes his protagonist's desire for an objective expert's evaluations of reality.

9. In both biographies of Percy, Samway's *Walker Percy: A Life* and Tolson's *Pilgrim in the Ruins*, the authors make note of his time in therapy with Janet Rioche.

10. Cash wants to dismantle the authority of this tradition, especially because of its racial and social paternalism, which supports a false hierarchy. To do so, he exposes the "mind of the South" and the "Southern way" of things. For instance, Cash asserts, "To sum up, the working code of the Old South, the code which really governed between the classes, was exactly adapted to the exigencies of the Southern order—was adapted above all to the old basic democracy of feeling—was itself, in its peculiar way, simply an embodiment of that feeling" (*Mind of the South* 41).

11. Unfortunately, in spite of his noble intentions, Will Percy, as is explained in Brannon Costello's book *Plantation Airs*, "participated in the subjugation, exploitation, and marginalization of Mississippi's black populace" (125).

12. Consider Mr. Vaught's Confederate Chevrolet dealership, where his salesmen wear "Reb-colonel hats and red walking canes" (*LG* 261).

13. To explore further the complicated issue of southern identity, read James C. Cobb's *Away Down South: A History of Southern Identity*.

14. *Adventures of Huckleberry Finn* is listed in the 2017 spring issue of *Oxford American: A Magazine of the South* as the fourth best southern novel, behind two of Faulkner's and Warren's *All the King's Men*.

15. Allen, *Walker Percy: A Southern Wayfarer* 61.

16. O'Gorman, "Walker Percy, the Catholic Church, and Southern Race Relations" 82.

17. O'Gorman opens his article on Percy and southern race relations by claiming that "literary critics of the past three decades . . . have devoted relatively little attention to [Percy's] treatment of . . . race" (67).

18. Allen claims, "D'Lo is probably Percy's nod to Faulkner's Disley, for Percy makes a point of having her notice the wall clock as she cooks and talks to will. Dilsey, a comforting presence in the Compson household, as D'Lo is in the Barretts . . ." (71).

19. Allen, *Southern Wayfarer* 66.

20. Ibid., 67.
21. Kobre, *Walker Percy's Voices* 97.
22. Goodman, "An Elegant Quest for Ordinariness" 20.
23. O'Gorman, "Walker Percy, the Catholic Church, and Southern Race Relations" 70.
24. There is a larger debate about whether Val is a model character. On the one side, there are scholars such as O'Gorman and Ciuba, who view her Catholic faith as the impetus for her altruistic choices. However, Costello argues that Val perpetuates the white-savior myth (*Plantation Airs* 143). Percy's intention, whether successful or not, was to juxtapose Val with her more self-absorbed family members.
25. Kierkegaard, "Of the Difference between a Genius and an Apostle" 93.
26. Ibid., 97, 99.
27. Ibid., 105.
28. Walker Percy to Caroline Gordon (April 6, 1962) from the papers of Ashley Brown, cited by Tolson, *Pilgrim in the Ruins* 300.
29. Burgess, *Ninety-Nine Novels* 100.
30. Desmond, *Walker Percy's Search for Community* 116.
31. Crews, "The Hero as 'Case.'"

CHAPTER THREE

1. In *The Moviegoer*, Binx mistakenly refers to his aesthetic way as his "Little Way," but this way of living was unfulfilling and oppositional to the Catholic way that he takes up at the end of *The Moviegoer*.
2. Granted, Binx's mother and Uncle Jules are Catholics, but he himself does not associate with the Roman Catholic Church for most of the novel. Therefore, I'm not counting him as one of Percy's "Catholic" heroes.
3. *Inferno* 1.1–3.
4. There are several allusions to Dante throughout this narrative. For example, when More has his epiphany about the lapsometer, he is lying in a hospital ward surrounded by "madmen moaning and whimpering like souls in the inner circle of hell" (*LIR* 28). Or, at the end of the book, Father Smith mentions the "outer circle of hell" (398).
5. Hobson, *Understanding Walker Percy* 81.
6. Cox, *The Secular City* 156.
7. In his library Percy owned at least ten books on or by Freud. And More compares the "first subject" of the Love Clinic to "Freud's first patient," linking Freud with the discussion (*LIR* 123).
8. Brooks, "Walker Percy and Modern Gnosticism" 680.
9. Douthat, *Bad Religion* 176.
10. Bloom, *The American Religion*.
11. Percy may have hidden a nice little piece of wit in the name of the pastor of

the American Catholic Church. Monsignor Schleikopf's name can be translated "Mr. Grinding Head." Percy knew German and would have purposefully chosen this word. If you read his name in conjunction with Proverbs 27:22, you have quite an indictment: "Though you grind a fool in a mortar, grinding the grain with a grinding head, you will not remove their folly." The congregants at St. Pius XII's Church (such as More's mother) are these grind-resistant fools.

12. Delbanco, *Death of Satan* 25.
13. Ciuba, *Walker Percy: Books of Revelations* 145.
14. Percy wants his novel to be cast in the light of Augustine. He writes to Foote: "What is [*Love in the Ruins*] about? Screwing and God (which all Catholic novels since Augustine have been about)" (*Correspondence* 147).
15. The last line of *Candide* is the hero's words, "Let us cultivate our garden" (169).
16. Harrison, *Gardens* 166.

CHAPTER FOUR

1. *Purgatory* 3.136–39.
2. Tolson, *Pilgrim in the Ruins* 404.
3. O'Connor, *Collected Works* 805.
4. The epigraph is from Lermontov, the Russian Romantic, regarding his protagonist of *A Hero of Our Time*.
5. O'Connor, *Collected Works* 806.
6. This confession is from a letter he wrote Foote on October 19, 1973 (*Correspondence* 179). However, both Tolson and Samway offer multiple references to similar letters written to various friends during this time in Percy's life.
7. Lancelot calls himself an "idler" (*Lancelot* 59). The label foreshadows his evil, for as it says in Proverbs 16:27, "Idle hands are the devil's workshop" (*The Living Bible*).
8. These names are all listed by Lancelot at various points in the novel. At the time that Percy was writing *Lancelot*, he was reading Foote's magnum opus on the Civil War and writing him letters about his account of Jefferson Davis, whom Percy called "Lucifer" (*Correspondence* 187). Although Margot is the one who asks Lancelot to play the part of "Jeff Davis," the tie hints at Percy's perspective on his character.
9. Lehmann-Haupt, "Camelot Lost," February 17, 1977.
10. Lancelot references the "mad Mansons" in his diatribe (*Lancelot* 160), but no critic or biographer that I have found has drawn the connection between these murders and Percy's story.
11. O'Donnell, *Augustine* 40.
12. Letter from Percy to Cheney, 1977, box 14, folder 21, Brainard Cheney Papers.
13. O'Connor, *Habit of Being* 143.
14. Ibid., 144.
15. Hobson, "'The Grand Inquisitor' and *Lancelot*," 119–30; Desmond, "Fyodor Dos-

toevsky, Walker Percy, and the Demonic Self," 88–107; Wilson, *Walker Percy, Fyodor Dostoevsky, and the Search for Influence.*

16. Lancelot repeats this "discovery" several times, most interestingly when he seems to substitute himself in God's place: "Was not that the new trait that people noticed about your Lord, that he spoke with authority?" (*L* 159).

17. Kreeft, *C. S. Lewis for the Third Millennium* 35.

18. Think too of Lancelot's "worm of interest" (*L* 21).

19. Percy seems to draw strongly from Lewis's novel for *Lancelot*. Just one example is when Screwtape warns Wormwood, "Do not think lust an exception. When the present pleasure arrives, the sin (which alone interests us) is already over" (77). And, Lancelot concurs: "Lust is a function of the future" (*L* 235).

20. Lewis, *The Screwtape Letters* 76.

21. Ibid., 75.

22. Percy, *More Conversations with Walker Percy* 10.

23. O'Gorman, "Confessing the Horrors" 135.

24. Hobson, *Understanding Walker Percy* 98.

25. In the preface to the paperback edition of *The Screwtape Letters*, Lewis admits, "[T]hough it was easy to twist one's mind into the diabolical attitude, it was not fun, or not for long. The strain produced a sort of spiritual cramp. The work into which I had to project myself while I spoke through Screwtape was all dust, grit, thirst, and itch. Every trace of beauty, freshness, and geniality had to be excluded. It almost smothered me before I was done. It would have smothered my readers if I had prolonged it" (183).

26. Weil, "Reflections on the Right Use of School Studies."

27. Dostoevsky, *The Brothers Karamazov* 260.

CHAPTER FIVE

1. Desmond, *Walker Percy's Search for Community* 181.

2. Isaiah 45:3.

3. Job 3:21.

4. Hobson, *Understanding Walker Percy* 110.

5. Taylor, *A Secular Age* 3.

6. Ciuba, *Walker Percy: Books of Revelations* 217.

7. In *Inferno* 27, Guido da Montefeltro relates to Dante how the demon and angel debated over to whom his soul belonged. This episode is repeated with a different conclusion over the soul of Montefeltro's son Buonconte in *Purgatorio*, 5.85–129.

8. Qtd. in Tolson, *Pilgrim in the Ruins* 423.

9. Barth, *Dogmatics in Outline* 75.

10. As a Catholic, Percy would have been familiar with the Stations of the Cross, in which Jesus falls three times. Barrett's three falls may be an attempt to align Percy's hero with Jesus.

11. Godshalk, "The Engineer, Then and Now" 36.
12. Ibid., 41.
13. Schwartz, "Will Barrett Redux?" 44.
14. Hobson, *Understanding Walker Percy* 109.
15. Tolson, *Pilgrim in the Ruins* 452.
16. De Mott, "'A Thinking Man's Kurt Vonnegut'" 81.
17. Tolson, *Pilgrim in the Ruins* 428.
18. Gilman, "Review of *The Second Coming*" 31.

CHAPTER SIX

1. Ciuba, *Walker Percy: Books of Revelations*, 257.
2. Desmond, *Walker Percy's Search for Community* 218.
3. O'Connor, *Habit of Being* 90.
4. This bent sword is reminiscent of Aunt Emily's letter opener in *The Moviegoer*. Binx Bolling "bent the tip trying to open a drawer" (*MG* 224). Similarly, More remembers that he "used to fiddle" with the sword at meetings in the rectory (*TS* 107).
5. Desmond, *Walker Percy's Search for Community* 25.
6. Ibid. For a deeper explanation of Percy's theory, read "Semiotic and a Theory of Knowledge" (*MIB* 243–64).
7. Desmond, *Walker Percy's Search for Community* 30.
8. Wertham, *A Sign for Cain* 155.
9. Qtd. in Tolson, *Pilgrim in the Ruins* 439.
10. Tolson, *Pilgrim in the Ruins* 444.
11. O'Connor, *Mystery and Manners* 96.
12. Dante is the quintessential Catholic poet. In *The Divine Comedy*, Dante the pilgrim circles around Mount Purgatory as he ascends. Similarly the movement toward God in Paradise is both cyclical and hierarchical. A more contemporary reference is Jeremy Begbie, who overturns the false dichotomy between linear and cyclical ideas of time with his attention to music, which moves toward resolution and then builds to a higher plane for the next repetitive sequence, exhibiting a rotating upward spiral (*Theology, Music, and Time* 110).
13. Julian of Norwich, *Revelations of Divine Love* 22. Joseph Schwartz makes a similar observation in his article on *The Second Coming* ("Will Barrett Redux?" 46).

APPENDIX

1. *MIB* 17.
2. In a 1979 letter to Foote, Percy is concerned about society's mass television consumption and wants to address it with his next project: "I still think there's a way of get-

ting at such things as the effect on a man of watching TV five hours a day for twenty years" (*Correspondence* 259).

3. Bartlett, "Walker Percy's Weirdest Book."

4. Correspondence with Rhoda Faust, November 4, 1981, qtd. in Samway, *Walker Percy: A Life* 360.

5. Correspondence with Bob Milling, qtd. in Samway, *Walker Percy: A Life* 361.

6. Percy writes Foote, September 10, 1980: "As you can see, this is not an entirely serious book, and yet it is serious" (*Correspondence* 270).

7. In his celebration of the thirty-year anniversary of the book, Alan Jacobs remarks, "[I]t may as well have been written yesterday" ("Percy and Sagan in the Cosmos").

8. John Sykes shows that "evidence against [Percy's] conclusion has mounted since his death. The research of Roger Fouts . . . indicates 'that chimps are capable of generating a symbolic world, including a universe of discourse where they can curse, tell lies, and make jokes'" (*Aesthetic of Revelation* 107). Although Percy hypothesizes that such a discovery will dethrone man (*LIC* 169), Sykes counters that these new findings do not refute Percy's theological assertions (*Aesthetic of Revelation* 108).

9. According to Percy, "[A]ll such triadic behavior is *social* in origin" (*LIC* 96).

10. "One such option is a sexual encounter. Another is war" (*LIC* 44).

11. Percy, "The Art of Fiction," interview with Zoltán Abádi-Nagy, *More Conversations with Walker Percy* 145.

12. Percy credits Kierkegaard's *Works of Love.*

13. Broyard, "Books of the Times."

14. Frank, "An Existential Guide."

BIBLIOGRAPHY

Allen, William Rodney. *Walker Percy: A Southern Wayfarer.* Jackson: University Press of Mississippi, 2006.
Amato, Elizabeth. "Walker Percy's Critique of the Pursuit of Happiness in *The Moviegoer, Lost in the Cosmos* and *The Thanatos Syndrome.*" *Political Companion to Walker Percy,* ed. Lawler and Smith. 47–68.
Auden, W. H. "The Unknown Citizen." *Another Time.* New York: Random House, 1940. www.poets.org/poetsorg/poem/unknown-citizen (accessed December 30, 2016).
Augustine. *Confessions.* Translated by Henry Chadwick. London: Oxford University Press, 1991.
Barth, Karl. *Dogmatics in Outline.* New York: Harper Perennial, 1959.
Bartlett, Tom. "Walker Percy's Weirdest Book." chronicle.com/blogs/percolator/walker-percys-weirdest-book/23835 (accessed June 2, 2015).
Begbie, Jeremy. *Theology, Music, and Time.* Cambridge, U.K.: Cambridge University Press, 2000.
Bloom, Harold. *The American Religion.* New York: Simon & Schuster, 1992.
Brainard Cheney Papers. Special Collections. Vanderbilt University Library.
Brooks, Cleanth. "Walker Percy and Modern Gnosticism." *Southern Review* 13.4 (October 1, 1977).
Brown, Peter. *Augustine: A New Biography.* HarperCollins, 2005.
Broyard, Anatole. "Books of the Times; Trying to Help the Self." *New York Times.* June 11, 1983. www.nytimes.com/1983/06/11/books/books-of-the-times-trying-to-help-the-self.html (accessed June 12, 2015).
Burgess, Anthony. *Ninety-Nine Novels: The Best in English Since 1939—Personal Choice.* New York: Simon & Schuster, 1984.
Caroline Gordon Papers. Manuscripts Division, Department of Rare Books and Special Collections, Princeton University Library.
Cash, W. J. *The Mind of the South.* New York: Vintage Books, 1991.
Ciuba, Gary. *Walker Percy: Books of Revelations.* Athens: University of Georgia Press, 2010.
Cobb, James C. *Away Down South: A History of Southern Identity.* New York: Oxford University Press, 2007.

Bibliography

Coles, Robert. "The Doubtful Pilgrim." *New York Times.* June 8, 1997.
———. *Walker Percy: An American Search.* Boston: Little Brown and Co., 1978.
Costello, Brannon. *Plantation Airs: Racial Paternalism and the Transformations of Class in Southern Fiction, 1945–1971.* Baton Rouge: Louisiana State University Press, 2007.
Cox, Harvey. *The Secular City.* New York: Macmillan, 1966.
Crews, Frederick C. "The Hero as 'Case.'" *Commentary,* September 1, 1966. www.commentarymagazine.com/articles/the-last-gentleman-by-walker-percy/ (accessed December 29, 2016).
Dahlstrom, Daniel O. *The Heidegger Dictionary.* London: Bloomsbury Academic, 2013.
Dante. *Inferno.* Trans. Anthony Esolen. New York: Modern Library, 2005.
———. *Purgatory.* Trans. Anthony Esolen. New York: Modern Library, 2004.
Delbanco, Andrew. *The Death of Satan: How Americans Have Lost the Sense of Evil.* New York: Farrar, Straus, and Giroux, 1995.
De Mott, Benjamin. "'A Thinking Man's Kurt Vonnegut': Review of *The Second Coming* by Walker Percy." *Atlantic Monthly,* July 1980: 81–84.
Desmond, John. "Fyodor Dostoevsky, Walker Percy, and the Demonic Self." *Southern Literary Journal* 44.2 (Spring 2012): 88–107.
———. *Walker Percy's Search for Community.* Athens: University of Georgia Press, 2010.
Dostoevsky, Fyodor. *The Brothers Karamazov.* Trans. Richard Pevear and Larissa Volokhonsky. New York: Farrar, Straus, & Giroux, 2002.
Douthat, Ross. *Bad Religion: How We Became a Nation of Heretics.* New York: Simon & Schuster, 2012.
Dreher, Rod. "Walker Percy Bourbon Tour." July 6, 2014. www.theamericanconservative.com/dreher/walker-percy-bourbon-tour-this-is-so-daddy/ (accessed May 18, 2015).
Dupuy, Edward J. *Autobiography in Walker Percy: Repetition, Recovery, and Redemption.* Baton Rouge: Louisiana State University Press, 1995.
Frank, Adam. "An Existential Guide For When You're Really 'Lost.'" National Public Radio, June 30, 2012. www.npr.org/2012/11/30/157305871/an-existential-guide-for-when-youre-really-lost (accessed December 29, 2016).
Gilman, Richard. "Review of *The Second Coming.*" *New Republic* 183.1–2 (July 5, 1980): 29–30.
Godshalk, W. L. "The Engineer, Then and Now; or Barrett's Choice." In *Walker Percy: Novelist and Philosopher,* ed. Gretlund and Westarp, 33–41.
Goodman, Walter. "An Elegant Quest for Ordinariness." LIFE. June 24, 1966.
Gretlund, Jan Nordby, and Karl-Heinz Westarp, eds. *Walker Percy: Novelist and Philosopher.* Jackson: University Press of Mississippi, 1991.

Bibliography

Harrison, Robert Pogue. *Gardens: An Essay on the Human Condition.* Chicago: University of Chicago Press, 2008.

Hobson, Linda Whitney. "'The Grand Inquisitor' and *Lancelot.*" *Walker Percy: Novelist and Philosopher.* In *Walker Percy: Novelist and Philosopher*, ed. Gretlund and Westarp, 119–30.

———. *Understanding Walker Percy.* Columbia: University of South Carolina Press, 1988.

Holy Bible, New International Version. Nashville, Tenn.: Cornerstone Bible Publishers, 1999.

Hooten, Jessica. "Individualism in Flannery O'Connor's *A Good Man Is Hard to Find.*" *Explicator* 66.4 (2008): 197–200.

Jacobs, Alan. "Percy and Sagan in the Cosmos." *Books and Culture*, March–April 2013. www.booksandculture.com/articles/2013/marapr/percy-and-sagan-in-cosmos.html?start=2.

John Paul II. "Letter to Artists." 1999. w2.vatican.va/content/john-paul-ii/en/letters/1999/documents/hf_jp-ii_let_23041999_artists.html.

Julian of Norwich. *Revelations of Divine Love.* New York: Penguin, 1999.

Kierkegaard, Søren. *Fear and Trembling.* Trans. with introd. by Alastair Hannay. New York: Penguin Classics, 1986.

———. "Of the Difference Between a Genius and an Apostle." *The Present Age* and *Of the Difference between a Genius and an Apostle.* Trans. Alexander Dru. Introd. Walter Kaufmann. Grand Rapids, Mich.: Harper Torchbooks, 1962.

———. *The Sickness Unto Death.* Ed. Howard V Hong. Princeton, N.J.: Princeton University Press, 1983.

———. *Works of Love.* Trans. with introd. and notes by Howard V. and Edna H. Hong. Princeton, N.J.: Princeton University Press, 1995.

Kobre, Michael. *Walker Percy's Voices.* Athens: University of Georgia Press, 2000.

Kreeft, Peter. *C. S. Lewis for the Third Millennium: Six Essays on The Abolition of Man.* San Francisco: Ignatius Press, 1994.

Lawler, Peter Augustine, and Brian A. Smith, eds. *A Political Companion to Walker Percy.* Lexington: University Press of Kentucky, 2013.

Lehmann-Haupt, Christopher. "Camelot Lost: *Lancelot* by Walker Percy." *Books of the Times*, February 17, 1977.

Lermontov, Mikhail. *A Hero of Our Time.* Trans. Nicolas Pasternak Slater. Oxford, U.K.: Oxford University Press, 2013.

Lewis, C. S. *Abolition of Man.* New York: HarperOne, 2015.

———. *The Screwtape Letters.* New York: Macmillan, 1961.

———. *Surprised by Joy: The Shape of My Early Life*. New York: Harcourt, Brace, Jovanovich, 1966.

———. *The Weight of Glory*. New York: HarperOne, 2001.

The Living Bible. www.biblegateway.com (accessed June 27, 2017).

Nash, Woods. "The Moviegoer's Cartesian Theater." *Political Companion to Walker Percy*, ed. Lawler and Smith. 29–46.

O'Connor, Flannery. *Collected Works*. Ed. Sally Fitzgerald. Ann Arbor: University of Michigan Press, 1988.

———. *The Habit of Being*. Ed. Sally Fitzgerald. New York: Farrar, Straus and Giroux, 1988.

———. *Mystery and Manners*. New York: Farrar, Straus and Giroux, 1962.

O'Donnell, James J. *Augustine: A New Biography*. New York: HarperCollins, 2005.

O'Gorman, Farrell. "Confessing the Horrors of Radical Individualism in *Lancelot*: Percy, Dostoevsky, Poe." *Political Companion to Walker Percy*, ed. Lawler and Smith, 119–44.

———. "Walker Percy, the Catholic Church, and Southern Race Relations." *Mississippi Quarterly* 53.1 (Winter 1999–2000): 67–88.

Percy, Walker. *Conversations with Walker Percy*. Ed. Lewis A. Lawson and Victor A. Kramer. Jackson: University Press of Mississippi, 1985.

———. "Introduction." *Lanterns on the Levee*. By William Alexander Percy. i–xviii.

———. "Introduction." *Walker Percy: A Comprehensive Descriptive Bibliography*. Ed. Linda Whitney Hobson. New Orleans: Faust Publishing Co., 1988.

———. *Lancelot*. New York: Farrar, Straus and Giroux, 1977.

———. *The Last Gentleman*. New York: Farrar, Straus and Giroux, 1966.

———. *Lost in the Cosmos: The Last Self-Help Book*. New York: Picador, 2000.

———. *Love in the Ruins*. New York: Farrar, Straus and Giroux, 1971.

———. *The Message in the Bottle*. New York: Farrar, Straus and Giroux, 2000.

———. *More Conversations with Walker Percy*. Ed. Lewis A. Lawson and Victor A. Kramer. Jackson: University Press of Mississippi, 1993.

———. *The Moviegoer*. New York: Random House, Inc., 1961.

———. *The Second Coming*. New York: Picador, 1999.

———. *Signposts in a Strange Land*. Ed. with an introd. by Patrick Samway. New York: Farrar, Straus and Giroux, 1991.

———. *The Thanatos Syndrome*. New York: Picador, 1999.

———, and Shelby Foote. *Correspondence of Shelby Foote and Walker Percy*. Ed. Jay Tolson. W. W. Norton & Co., 1997.

Percy, William Alexander. *Lanterns on the Levee: Recollections of a Planter's Son*. Introd. Walker Percy. Baton Rouge: Louisiana State University Press, 1973.

Bibliography

Quinlan, Kieran. *Walker Percy: The Last Catholic Novelist*. Louisiana State UP, 1998.

Samway, Patrick. "Two Conversations in Walker Percy's *The Thanatos Syndrome*: Text and Context." In *Walker Percy: Novelist and Philosopher*, ed. Gretlund and Westarp, 24–32.

———.*Walker Percy: A Life*. Chicago: Loyola University Press, 1999.

Schwartz, Joseph. "Will Barrett Redux?" In *Walker Percy: Novelist and Philosopher*, ed. Gretlund and Westarp, 42–53.

Smith, Brian. "Walker Percy's Last Men: *Love in the Ruins* as Fable of American Decline." In *Political Companion to Walker Percy*, ed. Lawler and Smith. 179–206.

Solzhenitsyn, Aleksandr. "A World Split Apart." Harvard University Commencement Address, June 8, 1978. www.americanrhetoric.com.

Sykes, John D., Jr. *Flannery O'Connor, Walker Percy, and the Aesthetic of Revelation*. Columbia: University of Missouri Press, 2007.

Tate, Allen. *Essays of Four Decades*. Wilmington, Del.: Intercollegiate Studies Institute, 1999.

Taylor, Charles. *A Secular Age*. Cambridge, Mass.: Harvard University Press, 2007.

"*The Thanatos Syndrome*: A Novel by Walker Percy." *Kirkus Reviews*. March 15, 1987. www.kirkusreviews.com/book-reviews/walker-percy/the-thanatos-syndrome/.

Thoreau, Henry David. *Walden*. New York: Thomas Y. Crowell & Co., 1910.

Tolson, Jay. *Pilgrim in the Ruins: A Life of Walker Percy*. New York: Simon & Schuster, 1992.

Voltaire. *Candide*. Irvine, Calif.: Xist Publishing, 2014.

Walker Percy Papers. Southern Historical Collection, Wilson Library, University of North Carolina–Chapel Hill.

Weil, Simone, "Reflections on the Right Use of School Studies." www.hagiasophiaclassical.com/wp/wp-content/uploads/2012/10/Right-Use-of-School-Studies-Simone-Weil.pdf.

Wertham, Frederic, MD. *A Sign For Cain: An Exploration of Human Violence*. New York: Macmillan, 1967.

Wilson, Jessica Hooten. *Walker Percy, Fyodor Dostoevsky, and the Search for Influence*. Columbus: Ohio State University Press, 2017.

Wiman, Christian. *Ambition and Survival: Becoming a Poet*. Port Townsend, Wash.: Copper Canyon Press, 2007.

Wyatt-Brown, Bertram. *The House of Percy: Honor, Melancholy, and Imagination in a Southern Family*. New York: Oxford University Press, 1996.

INDEX

Allen, William Rodney, 41–42, 137–38, 145
Amato, Elizabeth, 137, 145
America, 2, 4, 16, 39, 53, 55, 72, 82, 115
Americaness, percieved qualites of, 3, 16, 18, 20, 42, 53–56, 63, 65–66, 73, 82, 107, 112, 115, 126, 134, 136, 139–40, 145–46
Auden, W. H., 18, 136, 145
Augustine, 66–67, 77, 138, 140, 145

baptism, 14, 48–49, 51, 92
Barth, Karl, 96, 98, 141, 145
Bartlett, Tom, 143, 145
Begbie, Jeremy, 142, 145
Bible, 14, 46, 90, 140, 147
Bloom, Harold, 63, 139, 145
Brainard Cheney Papers, 78, 140, 145
Brooks, Cleanth, 62, 139, 145
Brown, Peter, 145
Broyard, Anatole, 134, 143, 145
Burgess, Anthony, 51, 139, 145

Caroline Gordon Papers, 14, 51, 137, 139, 145
Cartesian split, 22, 31, 36, 43, 46, 61, 126, 128, 130, 133, 136
Catholicism, and percieved qualities of, 13–16, 19, 28, 32–34, 47–50, 54–55, 58, 63, 67–68, 70, 72, 78, 82–83, 89, 102–4, 113, 120–21, 132, 138–42
Cash, W. J., 3, 39, 135, 138, 145
church, 4, 13–15, 17, 32, 34, 47–49, 55, 63, 68–70, 73, 78, 81–83, 85, 89, 93, 95, 97, 102–3, 108, 112–13, 119–21, 138–40
Ciuba, Gary, 65, 96, 105, 139–42, 145
Cobb, James C., 138, 145
Coles, Robert, 36, 136–37, 146
Costello, Brannon, 138–39, 146
Cox, Harvey, 56–57, 139, 146

Crews, Frederkick C., 139, 146

Dahlstrom, Daniel O., 136, 146
Dante, 56, 65, 70–72, 78, 83–85, 97, 139, 141–42, 146
Delbanco, Andrew, 64, 140, 146
demon, 64, 69, 73, 83–84, 97, 111, 141
demonic, 64–65, 67, 72–74, 83–86, 111, 141, 146
De Mott, Benjamin, 106, 142, 146
Desmond, John, 36, 81, 89, 107, 113, 137, 139–42, 146
devil, 56, 64–65, 67–68, 73, 77, 84, 108, 111–12, 140
Dostoevsky, Fyodor, 12, 34–36, 59, 65, 71, 73, 81–82, 115–16, 141, 146
Douthat, Ross, 63, 139, 146
Dreher, Rod, ix, 135, 146
Dupuy, Edward, 135, 146

existentialism, 18, 21, 36, 46, 96, 143, 146
eros, 17, 46, 60, 88, 104
Eucharist, 34, 55, 67–68, 108, 113, 120

Frank, Adams, 143, 146

Gilman, Richard, 106, 142, 146
Godshalk, W. L., 103–4, 142, 146
Goodman, Walter, 46, 137, 139, 146
Gretlund, Jan Norby, 146

Harrison, Robert Pogue, 69, 140, 147
Hobson, Linda Whitney, 57, 81, 86, 93, 105, 139–42, 147
Holy Bible, 147

Jacobs, Alan, 143, 147
John Paul II, 87, 147

151

Index

journey, 26, 30, 36, 39, 41, 43, 56, 71, 89, 133
Julian of Norwich, 122, 142, 147

Kierkegaard, Søren, 14, 19, 24, 27–28, 30, 32–34, 43, 46, 49–50, 70, 86, 93, 131–32, 135–37, 139, 143, 147
Kobre, Michael, 43, 139, 147
Kreeft, Peter, 82, 141, 147

language, 34, 39, 46, 79, 87, 89, 90, 100, 106, 110, 112–14, 117, 124, 126–27, 130
Lanterns on the Levee (Percy), 9, 30, 82, 135–37, 148
Lancelot (Percy), vii, xi, 36, 71–87, 89, 92–93, 96, 104–5, 121, 131, 140–41, 147–48
The Last Gentleman (Percy), vii, xi, 11, 36, 39, 41, 46, 49, 51–52, 58, 88, 91–95, 100, 102–3, 105, 148
Lawler, Peter Augustine, 147
Lehmann-Haupt, Christopher, 74, 140, 147
Lermontov, Mikhail, 140, 147
Lewis, C. S., 28, 84, 86, 137, 141, 147
Lost in the Cosmos: The Last Self-Help Book (Percy), vii, ix, xi, 10, 16, 22, 112, 123–24, 127, 131, 133–34, 136, 148
Love in the Ruins (Percy), vii, xi, 10, 53–54, 55–56, 58–60, 63–64, 67, 69–70, 74, 85, 102–3, 108–11, 136, 140, 148

marriage, 2, 4, 13, 59, 62, 79 , 88, 103, 105, 108–9, 131
The Message in the Bottle (Percy), xi, 90–91, 97, 112, 124, 126, 148
More Conversations with Walker Percy (Lawson and Kramer), 148, 33, 46, 86, 98, 107, 141, 143, 148
The Moviegoer (Percy), vii, xi, 9, 18, 23, 27, 34, 36, 41, 43, 45–47, 51, 57–58, 61, 75, 91–92, 101, 108, 136–39, 142, 148

O'Connor, Flannery, 14, 38, 54, 72, 78–79, 95, 110, 132, 136, 138, 140, 142, 148
O'Donnell, James J., 77, 140, 148
O'Gorman, Farrell, ix, 41–42, 47, 85, 138–39, 141, 148

Percy, Walker, ix, 1–19, 21–26, 28, 30, 32–43, 45–58, 60–67, 69–79, 82–92, 94–95, 97–98, 101, 104–9, 111–43, 148
Percy, William Alexander, 3–7, 30, 135–36, 148
pilgrim, 23, 56, 71, 82, 121, 132, 135–42
priest, 15, 33, 48–50, 64, 68–69, 72, 79, 85–87, 92–93, 103, 112, 114, 116–17, 119–22, 132

Quinlan, Kieran, 149

rotation, 1, 24–26
repetition, 24–26, 88, 112, 122
return, 1, 4, 12, 20, 23, 26, 29, 31, 41, 43–44, 61, 66–69, 84, 92, 101–2, 108, 121, 123, 129, 136
Roman Catholicism, 13, 15, 63, 69, 78, 89, 103, 120, 139

sacrament, 31, 34, 48, 67–68, 103, 113, 120
sacramental items and rituals, 48, 54, 59, 60, 85, 92, 102–3
saint, 17, 35, 45, 56, 67–68, 73, 80, 96, 116, 119–10, 122
salvation, 63, 71–72
salvific effects and visions, 11, 72, 108
Samway, Patrick, xi, 1–2, 135, 138, 140, 143, 149
saving (protecting), 76, 108, 134
Schwartz, Joseph, 105, 142, 149
science, 10–12, 22–23, 55, 63–66, 114, 123, 128, 131, 133
scientism, 64–65, 67, 94, 123
The Second Coming (Percy), vii, xi, 10, 44, 55, 61, 88–89, 91–93, 95, 98, 98, 100, 102–4, 106, 108, 122, 136, 142, 146, 148
self, 21–23, 26–28, 31, 36–39, 45, 48, 51, 62, 64, 67, 69, 75, 85, 110, 113, 117, 120, 123–34, 139, 141, 148
semiotic writings and thought, 113, 125, 130, 132, 142
Signposts in a Strange Land (Percy), xi, 15–16, 23, 29, 40, 54, 57, 61, 64, 66–67, 70, 114, 117, 133, 135–37, 148
Smith, Brian, 63, 149

Index

Solzhenitsyn, Aleksandr, 21, 136, 149
southerness, percieved qualities of, 3, 7, 9–10, 14, 26, 29, 36–37, 39–42, 44, 48, 74–76, 82, 87, 113, 115, 137–39, 145–46, 148–49
South, the, 2–5, 8, 15, 29–30, 36, 39–44, 47, 82, 94, 135, 137–38, 145–47
Sykes, John D., 143, 149

Tate, Allen, 37, 137, 149
Taylor, Charles, 94, 136, 141, 149
Thanatos, 17, 46, 60, 88, 104, 122
The Thanatos Syndrome (Percy), vii, xi, 2, 61, 107–8, 111–16, 119–20, 130, 135, 145, 148–49
Thoreau, Henry David, 20, 149
Tolson, Jay, xi, 1, 106, 136, 138–42, 148–49

Wayfarer, 3, 23, 43, 50, 55, 132, 138, 145
Weil, Simone, 87, 132, 141, 149
Wertham, Frederic, 114, 142, 149
Westarp, Karl-Heinz, 146
Wilson, Jessica Hooten, 141, 149
Wiman, Christian, 135, 149
Wyatt-Brown, Betram, 1, 134–36, 149

www.ingramcontent.com/pod-product-compliance
Lightning Source LLC
Chambersburg PA
CBHW020935230426
43666CB00008B/1692